The Assault on Universities

'The thoughtful papers collected in this important book represent a landmark intervention. They are essential reading for anybody seeking to understand the crisis in British education and the forces that produced it. Here is a timely and astute defence of the university that breaks free from the unimaginative pattern that can see education as only either a corporate or a private good. The manifesto shows what can be done to revive and expand our universities restoring their social mission.'

Professor Paul Gilroy, London School of Economics

'The corporatising of universal education is one of the most insidious and dangerous attacks on the very notion of human rights. This book calls us to arms. Every student, every educator who cares should read it.'

John Pilger

'This is an essential book. The future of our universities is up for grabs and the manifesto will play a huge role in providing alternatives at a time when the government says there aren't any.'

Clare Solomon, President of the University of London Union 2010–11 and co-editor of *Springtime* (2011)

'Universities are the new front line in the battle between the market and society. Students are being groomed for a life of debt on a learn-to-earn treadmill. Campuses are being commercialised at every turn. *The Assault on Universities* tells the story of what's happening to higher education, why and what we do about it.'

Neal Lawson, chair of Compass and author of *All Consuming* (2009)

'*The Assault on Universities* is a valuable contribution to ongoing global conversations about the possibilities of social, political and economic justice and the central role of cultural institutions and practices, especially education, in them.'

Professor Lawrence Grossberg, University of North Carolina at Chapel Hill

The Assault on Universities

A Manifesto
for Resistance

Edited by
Michael Bailey and Des Freedman

www.plutobooks.com

First published 2011 by Pluto Press
345 Archway Road, London N6 5AA

www.plutobooks.com

Distributed in the United States of America exclusively by
Palgrave Macmillan, a division of St. Martin's Press LLC,
175 Fifth Avenue, New York, NY 10010

British Library Cataloguing in Publication Data
A catalogue record for this book is available from the British Library

ISBN	978 0 7453 3192 8	Hardback
ISBN	978 0 7453 3191 1	Paperback
ISBN	978 1 84964 601 7	Kindle eBook
ISBN	978 1 84964 599 7	eBook PDF
ISBN	978 1 84964 600 0	ePub

Library of Congress Cataloging in Publication Data applied for

This book is printed on paper suitable for recycling and made from fully managed
and sustained forest sources. Logging, pulping and manufacturing processes are
expected to conform to the environmental standards of the country of origin.

10   9   8   7   6   5   4   3   2   1

Designed and produced for Pluto Press by Chase Publishing Services Ltd
Typeset from disk by Stanford DTP Services, Northampton, England
Simultaneously printed digitally by CPI Antony Rowe, Chippenham, UK and
Edwards Bros in the United States of America

Contents

Part IV   Student Politics

Part V   International Perspectives

Part VI   The Manifesto

1

An Introduction to Education Reform and Resistance

Des Freedman

'REFORM'

A celebrated education reformer noted recently that 'it is only when services are paid for that their beneficiaries really appreciate them and that their employees strive to perfect them. A world in which students pay for their own university education will be a world where the universities are better funded, intellectually freer and where economic justice ensures that the burden does not lie on the taxpayer but on graduates.'[1] Who issued this moving tribute to the market? Margaret Thatcher? Ronald Reagan? David Cameron? Nick Clegg? No, Terence Kealey, vice-chancellor of the University of Buckingham (fees: approximately £9000 per year), the UK's first private university and an institution that is 'proud never to have accepted Goverment [*sic*] funding, favouring instead our academic independence'.[2]

Kealey's words are significant because they so clearly articulate the ConDem coalition's devastating perspective on higher education policy as contained in the Browne Review on education funding and student finance and the government's own legislative programme of 2010–11. This includes a commitment to withdraw most public subsidies for universities, shift financial responsibility on to students who are now to be treated as customers, increase tuition fees to a level that an emerging market can sustain, re-package student debt and loans as 'deferred payments' and re-designate universities themselves as sites of service provision, consumer activity and commodity exchange. The UK's higher education system is to be transformed into a patchwork of academic supermarkets with, at one end, research-led Russell Group universities continuing to super-serve wealthier customers with a wide range of niche offerings while, at the other end, former Polytechnics in the Million+ group will be forced to clear their shelves of distinctive or idiosyncratic goods and to focus on those products for which there is already a clearly defined (mass) market. All shoppers, meanwhile, will have to pay higher prices.

This will be the state of British higher education in the second decade of the twenty-first century should the ConDem 'reforms' be fully implemented and internalised by universities themselves. It is a picture of renewed privatisation, intensive marketisation, rampant financialisation and a challenge to the very notion of the university as a mechanism for addressing social inequality and facilitating the circulation of knowledge whether or not it has immediate practical consequences. It is the substitution of private economic activity for robust public life. Of course universities are not, and never have been, pristine sites of autonomous intellectual labour – you only have to consider the close collaboration between many universities and the defence and security industries across the world. However, like many other publicly funded institutions which do not always live up to expectations (the BBC and the NHS spring to mind), a strong defence of the principle of public provision carries with it the possibility not only of 'holding the line' but also of invigorating and democratising these institutions. This involves both imagining and campaigning for policies that best express the public interest and most effectively protect it against those who are determined to place all areas of human activity under the discipline of the market.

Responding to the attacks on higher education, however, also requires an understanding of the various contexts behind the 'reforms'. According to the government, the most pressing challenge is the need to secure stable long-term funding for universities in the light of the budget crisis caused by what it describes as an unsustainable deficit caused by the previous Labour government's profligacy. What this means in practice is a decision to shift the burden of paying for higher education from the state to individual students. This is not a victimless crime. Research conducted by UCU has found that the scrapping of all public funding for the teaching of arts, humanities and social science subjects (as part of an 80 per cent cut to the annual block grant to universities), together with cuts of over £1 billion that have already been announced, means that some 40,000 jobs and 49 English universities are at risk.[3] The most vulnerable institutions are those teaching-intensive universities, often former polytechnics with the highest level of working-class students, who do not have the international students, research contracts or established 'brands' to help them withstand the removal of public funding.

This is, of course, only one small part of the government's neoliberal programme of privatisation and spending cuts which will see billions of pounds withdrawn from public services and welfare budgets as well as the devolution of power away from publicly accountable institutions to, for example, GPs in the running of the health service, academies in the provision of secondary education and housing associations in the management of social housing. We are therefore likely to see huge job losses affecting civil servants, NHS staff and council workers at precisely the time when unemployment, by the start of 2011, had already reached nearly 8 per cent with nearly one million young people without work, the highest since records began in 1992.[4] The government's scrapping of the Education Maintenance Allowance (EMA), originally aimed at improving participation rates in further education, will only compound the problem of youth unemployment.

Indeed, the government's determination to shrink the higher education budget is utterly counter-productive if it wishes to seek a way out of the recession. The UK already spends a lower proportion of its GDP on higher education (0.7 per cent) not only in comparison with EU and OECD averages (1.1 and 1 per cent respectively), but also in relation to a whole series of countries including the USA, Portugal, New Zealand, Iceland, Hungary and Mexico.[5] Now it wishes to reduce this even further even though its own policy documents are filled with rhetorical flourishes about the importance of higher education to the national economy and future prosperity. So while the Obama administration presses for an increase in its education and research budgets as a purposeful way to galvanise the US economy,[6] the UK government is set on gambling on the highly dubious assumption that private investment in education will deliver the same public benefits as state support.

The current attack on universities, however, should not be reduced to a desire simply to address the UK's current deficit, as many of the trends underlying the 'reforms' are far from new. Remember that it was a New Labour administration that first scrapped maintenance grants and introduced upfront charges in 1998; in 2003 then education secretary Charles Clarke insisted that '[a]s countries throughout the world have discovered, requiring students to contribute to the cost of their education is the only realistic alternative'.[7] Under New Labour, private sector activity in higher education grew from 32.3 per cent of all HE spending in 2000 to 64.2 per cent in 2007, well above the EU average of 20.6 per cent.[8] This huge increase in private finance was due not simply to the introduction of fees but to other initiatives such as the hundreds of millions of pounds of private investment under PFI schemes which were poured into capital projects on campuses, the government's backing of 'employer-led provision' and the granting of degree-awarding powers to private companies operating outside of the nationally agreed framework for higher education.

Universities are therefore increasingly subject to competing pressures: to continue to privilege teaching, learning and research as a public good but simultaneously to act as corporate entities in achieving this ambition (see Chapter 15 for an assessment of these tensions in relation to the USA). This is a highly unstable relationship as more and more of the structures of university life are outsourced and marketised. It is not simply about the Scolarest experience, where every cup of coffee tastes the same, but about the intrusion of private companies into the very fabric of academic life. Companies such as INTO and Kaplan, whose staff are on vastly inferior terms and conditions, are responsible for the recruitment and teaching of international students at a number of 'prestigious' universities including Exeter, East

Anglia and Sheffield, while education secretary David Willetts has made it clear that he wants to see more private providers operating in the HE sector. Welcoming the announcement by BPP University College that it would offer up to a thousand places on its programmes in law and business, Mr Willetts responded that '[w]e are seeing the first glimmerings of the opening of universities to supply-side reform'.[9]

Privatisation now extends well beyond the provision of catering and recruitment services. The ConDem's true objective may be to secure a fully-fledged market inside the UK higher education system but there are already a whole host of 'everyday' practices that seek to naturalise competition within academic life. The National Student Survey, where students rate their experience of teaching and resources (and for which an iPod is usually offered to one lucky student) is modelled on US approaches to 'customer satisfaction' in universities, while the impending Research Excellence Framework (REF), with its emphasis on bibliometrics and 'impact', is a further nod towards the instrumentalisation and quantification of higher education.

While respective governments have set the ideological and policy agenda, university employers seem reluctant to stand in their way. Many of those in the Russell Group positively embraced the Browne Review and the introduction of higher fees while very few vice-chancellors publicly declared their opposition to the government's 'reforms', leading one ex-VC to criticise his fellow employers for doing very little visibly to resist the cuts. 'Whatever view you take of the planned privatization of higher education, it [the silence of VCs] was not a stirring call to arms.'[10] Indeed, employers have been far more willing to use the premise of 'tough financial times' as an opportunity to seek redundancies (compulsory as well as voluntary) and drastic changes to pensions provision than they have been to stand up alongside staff and students in opposing the cuts.

So we now have a higher education system which is overwhelmingly privately financed and increasingly market-driven and an ideological consensus shared by all recent governments that this is both desirable and necessary. In this context, dreaming of a 'golden age' of universities is not a helpful campaign strategy. There can be no going back to a pre-ConDem 'paradise' given New Labour's commitment to privatisation. But there can also be no return to even older models of higher education given the enormous increase in student numbers and the justified reluctance to go back to a time where a university education was the preserve of a privileged minority. Instead, we need to look ahead: both to defend what is most progressive about the higher education system we have inherited and to imagine new policies, practices and structures for universities on which to focus our campaigns.

RESISTANCE

For many people, the march against tuition fee increases and funding cuts on 10 November 2010 marked the beginning of such a campaign. Staff and students had long been involved in specific battles, for example, against the withdrawal of funding for ESOL courses (English for speakers of other languages), against mass redundancies such as those at Leeds University in 2009/10 and in campaigns against the growth of the private sector in dozens of HE institutions. But more recent protests signal a movement that goes far beyond immediate questions of finance to engage with questions concerning the overall purpose of universities and their continued existence as sites of discussion and discovery. The media and indeed the leaders of the trade unions who called the November demonstration (the NUS and UCU) focused initially on the smashing of windows at Millbank, the headquarters of the Conservative Party. Quite quickly, however, it became clear that the determination of students, including school students who took to the streets in their tens of thousands towards the end of 2010, had captured the imagination of many others whose lives were set to be affected by the broad sweep of government cuts. The birth of a new student movement (see Part IV) has allowed millions to enter a debate about the legitimacy and ideological purpose of the ConDem spending cuts.

The breadth and imagination of this movement has helped partially to insulate it from the demoralisation that inevitably followed the passage of legislation confirming tuition fee increases and the abolition of the EMA in late 2010 and early 2011. This is set to be a struggle for the soul of universities that will be played out over years rather than months along with the pauses, setbacks and sudden advances that characterise most grass-roots campaigns. If resistance to the long-term, but now vastly accelerated, privatisation of universities is to be successful, then the campaign needs to operate on multiple fronts, to embrace a range of strategies and to involve the maximum number of people possible.

For many, the backbone of the movement to *defend* universities from further privatisation and to protect the livelihoods of those who work on campuses will be the higher education trade unions, the largest of which is the University and College Union (UCU), with over 120,000 members. The UCU has, in contrast to many other unions, actually grown since its creation in 2006 out of a merger between AUT (organized in the 'old' universities) and NATFHE (largely representing the post-1992 sector) and demonstrated its strength when members took industrial action in 2006 as part of a substantial pay claim, eventually winning a 15 per cent pay increase between 2006 and 2009 (a gain that employers seem reluctant to forget in current disputes). UCU has quickly established itself as a radical union, partly given the high-profile coverage of its conference resolutions in relation to a boycott of Israeli academic institutions, and partly because of the left-wing make-up of its National Executive Committee. Perhaps the key reason for its radicalism, however, is simply that its members find themselves in a fast-changing 'industry' where they are forced to act collectively in relation not only to 'bread and butter' issues (for example, massive casualisation, increased workloads and now deteriorating pay and pensions) but the more 'political' questions concerning curricula, research outcomes and, of course, the very 'idea' of the university.

At the time of writing, UCU members in HE are balloting for industrial action in defence of pensions, job security and salaries, rights which government and employers claim are unsustainable given the current economic problems. Clearly this is a question of priorities in the sense that billions of pounds of public money have been poured into UK banks since 2008 in recognition of their importance for the national economy. No such attention has been paid to UK universities, which are viewed instead as a drain on the public purse. Given the ideological nature of the attack on publicly funded universities, it therefore merits both a robust trade union response – serious and sustained industrial action that delivers a clear message to the employers – as well as a political response with demands on government (similar to those made by Aeron Davis in Chapter 5) in terms of raising taxes on the very rich and pursuing tax avoiders with greater vigour than is currently shown.

UCU members, however, will have to win not just ballots but support amongst other campus staff and students for their actions. This involves breaking down existing sectional barriers as far as possible (between professors and visiting tutors, between staff and students, between academics and support staff) through organising together, holding joint meetings and running united campaigns. Virtually every protest action in the last few years at Goldsmiths, for example, has been backed by both UCU and the Students Union including campaigns against INTO's proposal to recruit and teach international students, management's plans to set up a local Trust school free from local authority control and, of course, UCU's current industrial campaign against the attacks on pensions, jobs and pay. We run an annual teach-in together in which staff and students come together to discuss pressing themes – commodification, 'alternatives', the idea of a 'future' – and hold regular rallies sponsored by staff and student unions. The more we are encouraged to think of ourselves in the current circumstances as either service providers or customers, the more such unity will be essential in building successful campaigns.

But we also ought to go above and beyond trade union action that is often (and necessarily) defensive to consider ways in which we can use the site of the university as a space in which to consider and press for radical responses to the privatisation of higher education. Partly, this will help build union militancy but it is also an important way of legitimising our concerns and strategies inside the university itself. After all, why should discussions about the need to stand up to marketisation and rationalisation be kept off the agendas of departmental meetings? Who benefits from the separation of 'industrial' and 'political' issues apart from the employers? At Goldsmiths, when the tuition fee increases and spending cuts were first mooted in 2010, we held a series of emergency *departmental* meetings with students in order to voice our concerns and to listen to theirs; we have since launched the 'Radical Goldsmiths' initiative, backed by several academic departments as well as campus unions, which will host a series of events and also attempt to rediscover the now nearly-forgotten radical past of the university through oral history interviews and archive research.

We also need to recognise that the movement has thrown up a vast number of imaginative forms of struggle that can help to foster a mood of resistance and to draw in ever greater numbers. The occupations of the National Gallery and Sothebys by members of Arts against Cuts seeking to demonstrate the intellectual vandalism of ConDem policies were inspired by the dozens of occupations that swept campuses in 2010 (see Chapter 12). At the time of writing, students are occupying the London School of Economics in protest at the university's acceptance of £1.5 million from the Libyan regime, with one student arguing that 'LSE has the most market-driven fund-raising model there is in the UK. Has that model reduced them into a simple gun for hire?'[11] Activists from the University of Strategic Optimism have followed the example of the UK Uncut campaign in occupying banks and holding public meetings about the origins of the debt, while thousands of university and school students are preparing to engage in the next day of action against the tuition fee rises.

This is a disparate, energetic, passionate and at times confused movement and yet one that has most visibly highlighted the mood for resistance that exists throughout the UK. The ConDem's assault on universities has triggered a more general anger about the legitimacy of the government's spending cuts and a real concern about their impact on the future of jobs, public services and welfare provision. Those of us who work in universities or who are prospective or current students are faced with the prospect of being part of a much broader coalition of resistance against the government's determination to shrink the state and, following the turmoil of the financial crisis, to restore profitability and confidence to their friends in business. But we also have another responsibility: to defend the idea of university education as a public good that is reducible neither to market values nor to instrumental reason. Attack is often the best form of defence, and this book is a contribution not simply to thinking about how best to preserve what we have in higher education but to demand much more. We may well need industrial action, rallies, marches, occupations, teach-ins and teach-outs to defeat the transformation of our campuses into cost centres and ideological supermarkets. But we will also need a clear vision of what the university should be: a public service, a social entitlement, a space for critical thinking and a place of discovery.

NOTES

1. Terence Kealey, *Independent*, 16 February 2011.
2. University of Buckingham website, available at http://www.buckingham.ac.uk/admissions/fees [accessed 21 February 2011].
3. UCU, *Universities at risk: the impact of cuts in higher education spending on local communities* (UCU: London, 2010), p. 3.
4. Harry Wallop, 'Youth unemployment hits record', *Daily Telegraph*, 16 February 2011.
5. OECD, *Education at a Glance 2010* (Paris, OECD, 2010), table B2.4.
6. Christine Armario, 'Obama's new budget increases education spending amid nationwide cuts', *Huffington Post*, 15 February 2011. Available at: http://www.huffingtonpost.com/2011/02/15/obama-education-budget_n_823735.html [accessed 21 February 2011].
7. Charles Clarke, *HoC Debates*, 22 January 2003, column 305.
8. OECD, *Education at a Glance*, table B3.2b.

9. Quoted in Chris Cook, 'Private providers to offer university places', *Financial Times*, 17 August 2010.
10. Peter Scott, 'And so farewell to my "stakeholders"', *Education Guardian*, 22 February 2011, p. 3.
11. Quoted in Ian Cobain et al., 'Leader's LSE-educated son no longer a man the west can do deals with', *Guardian*, 22 February 2011, p. 6.

Part I

The Changing Idea of the University

2

The Idea of the University

John K. Walton

In May 2008 an editorial in *Subtext*, the unofficial on-line newsletter of Lancaster University, lamented that 'Modern academics ... have to fight just to preserve the integrity of their vocation, protect their necessary freedoms and democratic interests, and be constantly vigilant just ... to preserve the conditions for the sort of intellectual pursuits and disputes in which they would much rather be engaged.'[1] Lancaster is a leading research university in the United Kingdom, but it clearly suffers from its share of the widespread discontents among academics which have their counterparts throughout the British education system, and elsewhere.

An illustration of current problems and conflicts can indeed be located on the Lancaster University website, where the Innovation and Enterprise Unit, residuary legatee of the School of Independent Studies, is still accessible in February 2011, despite its closure (shortly ahead of the Department of Continuing Education), also in 2008. Its staff were transferred or made 'redundant'. When Independent Studies was formally established in 1973, it was the first such initiative in Britain. Its five key principles were: student responsibility for learning, deep learning, critical thinking, transferable skills, and freedom of learning experience. Basically, it allowed students to construct their own themed degrees, including research elements, with appropriate guidance and supervision. But instead of this imaginative innovation being celebrated within the university, it was always under siege, although the repeated academic reviews to which it was subjected always reported enthusiastically. It was interdisciplinary, untidy and hard to 'manage', and it did not fit the university's structures. And, eventually, Lancaster threw it away, despite its efforts to engage with commerce as well as community. At the turn of the millennium it became the Innovation and Enterprise Unit, whose rhetoric tried to conciliate changing times, as it offered a BA in Consultancy and Independent Research which was geared up to improving employability (that Holy Grail of the twenty-first century education system) by 'working with a client resolving *real* (author's italics) issues and problems'. It is not clear whether academic issues and problems were regarded as unreal or surreal, but even this business-friendly transformation and presentation did not save the unit. Its demise reflected a much wider *malaise*, which we shall now explore.[2]

The statement in *Subtext* is, as Ronald Barnett would point out, ideological.[3] Words such as 'integrity', 'vocation', 'necessary freedoms' and 'democratic interests' are highly charged and loaded with assumptions, which are in opposition to the invading ideologies of entrepreneurism, competition and managerialism, of accountability and audit, of narrow pseudo-practical vocationalism, comparability, standardisation, measurement and the construction of league tables. *Subtext* assumes that university teachers and researchers should have an almost priestly vocation, an attachment to academic activity as a value and an end in itself. This will lead them to work unsupervised without counting the hours, while nurturing students and pursuing their duties in careful, ethical pursuit of the advancement of knowledge, without agenda-setting or other interference from without, in an environment where policy is made and change managed through academic debate based on reasoned, inclusive discussion among a community of scholars. This is entirely compatible with a secularised rendering, a century and a half later, of John Henry Newman's *The Idea of a University*. To remove the transmission of Catholic truth from his agenda might be thought to tear its heart out, but his commitments to a university as a school of universal learning, the communication and circulation of thought, the pursuit of mutual education in every kind of knowledge, and in a setting where 'inquiry is pushed forward, and discoveries verified and perfected ... and error exposed, by the collision of mind with mind, and knowledge with knowledge', are very close to the aspirations articulated in *Subtext*. So is the idea that 'the professor is a missionary and a preacher ... pouring (his science) forth with the zeal of enthusiasm'. The antithesis of Newman's vision of a university was utilitarianism, narrow training for the workplace, rote learning, line management from the 'top' down, or the fragmentation of knowledge into sealed compartments. It is safe to say that he would have liked the principles that underlie Independent Studies.[4]

Shorn of their Catholic and anti-secular dimensions, and mediated through the overlapping ideas of Matthew Arnold, such preconceptions about what a university, and university teaching, should be were still very much alive when the present writer began his academic career, at that same University of Lancaster, in the early 1970s, and it is reassuring to find that their proponents still fight on. Not that this, or even the dawn of the Robbins era in the 1960s, was a Golden Age, and it can appear so only in the light of subsequent developments. There had been plenty for people to protest about in 1968, when university administrations' propensity for the arbitrary and repressive suspension of due process became only too apparent under challenge, and in 1970 Edward Thompson denounced 'Warwick University Limited'.[5] A system based on trust allowed some people to do very little, while the cultivation of a reputation for administrative incompetence enabled necessary tasks to be funnelled disproportionately towards the willing and responsible. Policies might be debated and voted on at Senate or Board of Studies, but departmental administration could be oppressive. Lancaster's 'Craig Affair' in the early 1970s saw a colleague threatened with dismissal, and eventually shunted into internal exile as an 'Extra-Departmental Teaching Officer', for alleged Marxist bias in his teaching and assessment, an episode which highlighted problems on both sides.[6] Students were not always clear about expectations or assessment, and some decidedly eccentric practices were allowed to flourish. But Lancaster never approached the insouciance of an Oxford without (in History, in the late 1960s) prescribed lecture courses or reading lists, except where conscientious individual tutors provided them, and with an assessment system based on unseen final exams which in some subjects included material which had been 'taught' in the first year. And (for example) Lancaster did allow the present writer to supervise an excellent Independent Studies major on the decline of morris dancing in the Victorian South Midlands, which was examined by the director of the Institute of Historical Research (who raised the marks), and was eventually expanded to form an impressive scholarly book.[7] Even then, there were worries about seeming to award degrees in morris dancing, and the possible reactions of the tabloid press (hence the recruitment of the urbane and judicious Professor Michael Thompson as external examiner); but some of us still believe that this kind of activity is self-evidently worthwhile.

The creativity, originality and depth of research fostered by Independent Studies at its best would now be hard to re-create; and the persistence of such values within university systems everywhere has been systematically undermined, especially since the 1990s and with accelerating force in the twenty-first century, by a creeping importation of monocultural management values which have systematically attacked core academic ideals, ostensibly in the interests of transparency, competitiveness and the demonstration of 'value for money' under the destructive rubric of the 'New Public Management' and associated innovations.[8] This might be interpreted as the late arrival of a universal 'modernisation process' at a particularly recalcitrant set of institutions, but it might also be seen as the unjustified and distorting extension of market-dominated assumptions into one of many inappropriate areas where their consequences are destructive. Since 1998, especially, with the introduction of the 'Transparency Review', followed in short order by Time Allocation Surveys and (from 2005) the allocation of 'Full Economic Costing' to research projects, government-driven attempts to quantify, cost and compare all aspects of academic activity have proliferated. But the process had deeper roots, and already in 1993 Shore and Roberts were arguing that the development of quality assurance systems was turning the higher education system into a panopticon, with teachers and researchers as the closely observed, classified, contained and controlled prisoners distributed along its corridors.[9] They understood that the results of such attempts to measure the immeasurable would sap academic standards, by reducing legitimate activity to what seemed amenable to measurement, but the time wasted in filling out endless forms, and the anxiety generated thereby, made negative contributions of their own. And the introduction of external observers not only altered the nature of what was observed, but also distorted it by stimulating inaccurate reporting. The Transparency Review and time allocation surveys made the insulting assumption (consistent with an assembly-line mentality) that all academics worked a 37.5-hour week. Those who worked much longer hours, out of interest, a sense of professional duty or sheer pressure of work, could not know which hours to include and exclude. This made nonsense of percentage allocations of time, an argument to which the system's administrators were impervious, and for many people the only way to deal with the complex and intrusive demands of the form, with its impossibly precise classifications of the use of time, was to make the answers up. This in turn conjured up the spectre of future historians of higher education using this 'evidence' as if it were a trustworthy reflection of reality. Worse still, it transpired that at institutional level there was a (secret) 'right answer' to the imagined division of working time, and that collective deviation from it would have financial consequences.[10]

Such monitoring formed part of a much wider culture of quantification, target-setting and league table construction, with associated game-playing and neglect of unlisted objectives, which extended across the whole education system and far beyond, beginning with school league tables following the 1987 election manifesto of Thatcher's Conservatives, but spreading inexorably under 'New Labour'. As Robert J. Graham presciently forecast in 1989, this was Robert Lowe's 'Revised Code' of the 1860s revisited, promoting 'teaching to the test', the reduction of content and assessment to what could apparently be measured and compared, and the hollowing out of everything that was stimulating or creative. As Matthew Arnold, whose job it was to administer that system, noted in 1867, this reliance on 'mechanical processes' gave a 'mechanical turn' to school teaching. He also noted the high cost of setting up and running such mechanisms for comparison, reward and punishment, which always becomes a problem when imaginary markets are constructed, managed and fine-tuned by proliferating bureaucratic armies.[11] By the end of the twentieth century this revived Revised Code virus had worked through the system from tests at 7, 11 and 14 to infect A-Level, reducing much learning to bite-sized assessment exercises and penalising initiative and originality, which compromised the apparent integrity of universal individual comparability. Education was sacrificed on the altar of competition: it was more important that students should seem to have a level playing field for assessment (with an infinity of complex adjustments in practice) than that their personal and social development should be furthered by interesting, flexible, diverse curricula and teaching methods. And there was an ever-present temptation to seek 'soft' and apparently 'mainstream' options which minimised risk to outcomes and league table positions. The dominant ideology, under Blair as under Thatcher (and Major), was an almost religious faith in markets and competition, which paid no heed to the existing wealth of understanding and experience in academe and the labour movement, and took as its sole aim the materialist goals of preparing students for the corporate labour market. Mr Gradgrind was triumphant, and his name was even more evocative than Dickens had intended.[12]

Even where the universities themselves, or departments within them, were able to resist these pressures, there were knock-on effects. They had to work harder to bridge the widening gap between the expectations of sixth form and those of university. And siren voices advocating similar changes to assessment systems were swelling in seductive chorus. But the greatest evil here was the rise of a narrow, utilitarian vocationalism – the notion that the only conceivable purpose of going to university is to get the right sort of corporate job, so that universities become the training wings of international corporations, supported partly by the taxpayer (so not by the corporations, who pay only token levels of tax), but paid for increasingly by the students themselves. The corollary of this was the denial of any notion that education was about personal development in a wider sense, the pursuit of understanding, humanity and enlightenment for their own sake, which had enlivened the tradition of adult education in the humanities for a century, and still endured within many universities. Here 'New Labour' privileged the narrow, practical vocationalist preference of the party's pragmatic Fabian social engineering tradition, completing the destruction of the 'Great Tradition' in adult education by pricing non-vocational classes at full 'market' rates, and developing an emergent trend of the 1990s by insisting on the formal assessment of so-called 'leisure learning'.[13] This ideology had become all-pervading in the Mandelson and Browne reports on higher education, which saw the purpose of universities as the inculcation of skills for a corporate business environment. Meanwhile, within the state schools the pressure increased for students, from the age of 14 onwards, to identify a 'career' and construct their educational (or training) programme to prepare for it, at a transitional stage in personal development when students were unequipped to make such 'choices'. Within the universities, competition and assessment marginalised personal development, creativity and even (sometimes) originality. An extraordinary paranoia developed around the punitive enforcement of deadlines and attendance, which was directed, paradoxically, at legal (at 18) adults who were paying for their own degrees, rather than the under-21 minors who had received grants in the previous generation, and who had not been policed in these obsessive, controlling ways, which imposed their own burdens on academic staff and institutional costs.

The rise of McKinseyism, the doctrine that things that cannot be measured have no value, has been even more damaging. An example of its workings in practice was the Dean of Arts and Humanities' justification of the closure of Middlesex University's unique Philosophy Department on the grounds that, though prestigious (and successful), it made 'no measurable contribution' to the university.[14] In university research the McKinsey mentality has created target cultures and false indicators to further the construction of league tables based on arbitrary, loaded criteria which encourage collusion and game playing. The incorporation of 'impact factors', based essentially on market criteria and the values of 'Britain's Got Talent' into the successor Framework to the Research Assessment Exercise was dissected magnificently by Stefan Collini, but his demolition of this absurd and sinister proposal made no discernible impact on policy. It could not be answered, but it could be ignored.[15] More generally, the proposed change of emphasis in research evaluation (and remuneration) from peer review to 'metrics' enhanced and extended the privileged status of calculations of quality and impact that were based on league tables of academic journals, using citation indices and compiled by private companies. The lack of rigour and relevance in these compilations, and their systematic biases towards orthodoxy, the English language, and the 'big battalions' (especially in Economics, where heterodox theory and alternative business models are systematically excluded from the 'leading' publications),[16] have been thoroughly exposed by critical bibliometricians.[17] So has their bias against the humanities and some social sciences, where the 'gold standard' is the book-length monograph, and chapters in books are an important outlet, but neither publication mode is recognised by the league table compilers.[18] But these deceptively simple evaluation systems are convenient for managers, who can use them to bully academics into publishing in the 'right' journals; while academics in their turn are tempted to follow 'hot' topics which generate citations, and discouraged (or even forbidden) from performing necessary but less visible roles such as editing, enabling or writing book reviews, and even sitting on editorial boards. Such values also imperil recruitment to the external examiner system, whose effective functioning is important to quality control, but which is also poorly paid and increasingly mired in bureaucracy. The system thus discourages originality and interdisciplinarity (especially when they are slow to generate citations: instant gratification is required), and crowds out necessary academic services which are invisible to it.

In many cases the assumed virtues of exposure to 'market discipline' associated with the 'New Public Management', and of which these developments are part and parcel, have led universities to behave as if they were public limited companies, operating under the rubric of 'shareholder value' that spread like a toxic virus from the United States in the 1990s. This enshrined the doctrine that the sole duty of a company was to maximise the financial return to its shareholders, as anticipated and exemplified by the sustained efforts of one asbestos giant over half a century to avoid paying compensation to its workers who suffered from industrial diseases, on the assumption that protecting its profits was more important.[19] Responsibility for the proper stewardship of taxpayers' money, under increasingly rigorous, expensive and time-consuming bureaucratic scrutiny, was increasingly interpreted purely in financial terms by managers who had often been imported from beyond the academic world. As the philosopher Jonathan Wolff has pointed out, the attack on Philosophy at Middlesex is part of this story: it brought in a lower per capita income on current 'banded' government funding policy, and therefore seemed uneconomical. As Wolff also noted with some relish, that policy has now been changed, and apparently, 'Middlesex made a spectacular miscalculation'.[20] How, incidentally, can you have a university without philosophers, and (the logical conclusion) without the humanities?

All this reflects the increasingly sacred status of the 'business plan', which can be manipulated to set aside and destroy those aspects of a university with which management are uncomfortable, threatening to destroy the knowledge base of unfashionable subjects. Such policies are furthered by the development of a new cadre of academic 'managers', especially in the post-1992 universities where heads of department, deans and pro-vice-chancellor posts are no longer responsibilities undertaken for the good of the academic community, but stepping stones on a management career ladder, part of a process of taking appropriate staff development courses and receiving indoctrination in management theory. Some managers stay in touch with research and teaching issues, but every university has others who have adopted management as a career with higher financial rewards than research and teaching, especially for those whose academic profiles were less than inspiring. Such people are probably much more prevalent in the post-1992 establishments, where this career model is entrenched. Their colleagues and underlings know who they are, but the reputation for power of the libel laws in England makes it impossible to provide specific examples. Such people have chosen to trade in academic values for those of 'management'. They are line managers, and they pass management decisions on down the chain. These are often the people who betray the idea of the university from within.

An extension of the process is the importation of management from outside the university sector, bringing in people whose only values and experience are commercial, and who have no idea of academic worth or merit. A single illustration must suffice. As an assessor for a personal chair in History at a new university in 2009 I was greeted by an externally recruited senior manager who was worried about the candidate's low profile on the Linkedin business networking site, which might prejudice his suitability for a chair.[21] She could not understand the assessors' laughter, but this is no joke. It displays a culture in which deans head up their public profiles with ephemeral media contributions, and leave anything of residual academic substance parked in backwaters. And these are the people who 'manage' universities.

So British universities have become vehicles for the further development of corporate capitalism, whose real and present threat to diversity of all kinds extends to universities as well as tropical rain forests, as it prizes measurable growth, a quick fix and the bottom line. Ironically, at the level of whole societies the 'private enterprise' of corporate capitalism is grossly *inefficient*, apart from maximising profits for individual companies and seeking routes to oligopoly and monopoly through the corruption of the political process. Late capitalism has no interest in the wider systems through which people live their lives, and does not cost the multiplication of individual delays, wasted time and inconvenience that follows from (for example) closing post offices and extending counter queues in pursuit of a profit-based business model. It abhors genuinely critical thinking, outside its box. As it invades the universities, it drives out the spirits of Newman and Arnold, and intrudes the infelicitous calculus of Jeremy Bentham and Edwin Chadwick. Resistance is growing, but by its nature it fights local battles, backs to the wall. The question is: how to organise effectively on a broader front to further the survival, and revival, of real universities in an utterly philistine political environment.

NOTES

1. Editorial in *Subtext* 37, 1 May 2008, http://www.lancs.ac.uk/subtext/archive/issue037.htm [accessed 12 February 2011]. The Subtext archive offers an excellent sustained critical commentary on the current state of higher education in England.

2. http://www.lancs.ac.uk/depts/indstud/ [accessed 12 February 2011]; http://www.lancs.ac.uk/subtext/archive/issue036.htm [accessed 12 February 2011].

3. Ronald Barnett, *Beyond All Reason: Living with Ideology in the University* (Milton Keynes: Open University Press, 2003).

4. Ian Ker, *John Henry Newman: A Biography* (Oxford: Oxford University Press, 1988), Chapter 9.

5. M.A. Rooke, *Anarchy and Apathy* (London: Hamish Hamilton, 1971), for an unsympathetic account; E.P. Thompson, *Warwick University Ltd.* (Harmondsworth: Penguin, 1970).

6. Council for Academic Freedom and Democracy, *The Craig Affair* (London: CAFD, 1972).

7. Keith Chandler, *The Social History of Morris Dancing in the English South Midlands, 1660–1900* (Enfield Lock: Hisarlik, 1993).

8. R. Deem, S. Hillyard and M. Reed, *Knowledge, Higher Education and the New Managerialism* (Oxford: Oxford University Press, 2007).

9. C. Shore and S. Roberts, 'Higher Education and the panopticon paradigm: Quality Assurance as "disciplinary technology"', *Higher Education Review* 27 (3) (1993), pp. 8–17.

10. These comments are based on the author's experience as a research manager in a British university between 1998 and 2007.

11. Robert J. Graham, 'Arnold and Thatcher: a report on contemporary education policy', *McGill Journal of Education* 24 (1989), pp. 69–80.

12. Eric E. Robinson, 'Blair's legacy in education', http://socialisteducation.org.uk/EricR_EP97 [htm accessed 25 February 2011].

13. Tom Steele, *The Emergence of Cultural Studies* (London: Lawrence and Wishart, 1997).

14. http://www.corporatewatch.org.uk/?lid=3603 [accessed 26 February 2011].

15. S. Collini, 'Impact on humanities', *Times Literary Supplement* 13 November 2009; John Stone to editor, *TLS* 18 November 2009.

16. F.S. Lee, 'The Research Assessment Exercise, the state and the dominance of mainstream economics in British universities', *Cambridge Journal of Economics* 31 (2007), pp. 309–25; P. Kalmi, 'The disappearance of cooperatives from economics textbooks', *Cambridge Journal of Economics* 31 (2007), pp. 625–47.

17. É. Archambault and V. Larivière, 'History of the Journal Impact Factor: contingencies and consequences', *Scientometrics* 79 (2009), pp. 639–53.

18. É. Archambault and V. Larivière, 'The limits of bibliometrics for the analysis of the social science and humanities literature', *World Social Science Report. Knowledge Divides* (Paris: UNESCO and ISSC, 2010), pp. 251–4.

19. Paddy Ireland, 'Financialization and corporate governance', *Northern Ireland Legal Quarterly* 60 (2009), pp. 1–34; Geoffrey Tweedale, *From Magic Mineral to Killer Dust* (Oxford: Oxford University Press, 2001).

20. Jonathan Wolff, 'Why masterful inactivity wins the day', *Guardian Education*, 22 February 2011.

21. He was awarded the chair, just in time. Here as elsewhere, internal promotions on academic merit were subsequently abolished. Henceforward promotion was only for 'managers'.

3

What is a University Education For?

Neil Faulkner

Politicians are unanimous about the role of universities in providing the knowledge and skills demanded by British capitalism as it attempts to compete in an increasingly crowded world market. Manifestos, policy statements and speeches have little or nothing to say about what the Americans call 'the liberal arts' and the British 'the humanities'. These, it seems, are luxuries we can ill afford, indulgences we regard with pained expressions, as we focus on the dizzy possibilities of the digital economy. What is the value of being able to date Roman pottery, read medieval Latin or read a Victorian novel? What has that got to do with devising new financial derivatives or designing improved weapons systems? How does it improve our skill set, raise our productivity and increase our GDP?

You can see the impact of the erosion of the ideal of 'universal' education by comparing the typical campus of the 1970s with that of today. It was only the fag-end of a student revolt that had peaked in the late 1960s. But attending a traditional university at the end of the 1970s was still to enter a hubbub of radical activity and debate. There were pickets, occupations and rent strikes against investments in companies operating in apartheid South Africa. There were several left-wing meetings organised by political parties and campaign groups every week. Wall space was plastered with notices for them. It was possible to be a full-time political activist. I sometimes had to have 'breakfast meetings' to plan the next demo and was too busy to attend lectures during my final two years. It was, I now realise, only the fag-end. But at the time, we expected the revolution soon.

The contrast, going into a 'new university' at the end of the noughties, could not have been more stark. The austere glass-

and-concrete edifices of the Ages of Major and Blair stand testimony to the success of the neoliberal counter-revolution. Entombed within, breathing only the stale air of an 'academy' from which all critique and counter-culture has been virtually eradicated, are the proto-proletarians of a digitised, 'knowledge-based' capitalism. To enter the main campus complex of the University of Hertfordshire – to take my local example – is like entering the atrium of a City bank. There is the same numbing brainlessness, the same suffocating absence of thought and imagination, the same absoluteness about the unquestioning conformity. So drained of intellect, culture, and politics are they that many of these places are the very negation of 'universities'. There is nothing 'higher' about them. They are skills factories turning out labour units in an environment that combines the clinical functionalism of Huxley's *Brave New World*, the political conformity of Orwell's *1984*, and the bureaucratic absurdity of Kafka's *The Trial*.

Is the contrast overdrawn? If it is, the procedure remains valid. We seek to understand the world by abstracting essences and tendencies from the more messy and multilayered social reality we actually experience. What Chris Harman has called 'the fire last time' – the explosion of political and social revolt during the years 1968–1975 [1] – created a ferment of critique and democracy. This infected especially the young and the universities and, by doing so, it brought the universities closer to their ideal. For the very essence of 'universal' education is that it unites practice and theory, skills and critique, the knowledge necessary to do things with an understanding of purpose and consequence.

This defines the contradiction at the very heart of the bourgeois academy. It is a contradiction that first arose in response to what historian Eric Hobsbawm calls the 'dual revolution' of the late eighteenth century: the combination of the economic or 'industrial' revolution pioneered in Britain from *c*.1750 with the political or 'bourgeois' revolution whose most radical expression was in France between 1789 and 1794.[2] But the contradiction became explosive only in the two decades after the Second World War with the expansion of higher education in that period. And it has become yet more explosive today after a further four decades of expansion, during which the number of university students in Britain has quadrupled. To grasp its profundity, it is useful to place this contradiction in a deep-time historical context.

The bourgeois university has its roots in the gymnasia, academies and libraries of Ancient Greece. The preserves of a leisured elite, these offered a curriculum that combined literature, science, philosophy and physical training. Uncontaminated by any discordant plebeian presence, the Greek 'universities' developed as part of a wider elite reaction against democracy. Mass participation in the politics of the city-states, achieved through a series of 'hoplite revolutions' during the sixth and fifth centuries BC, was bloodily suppressed by an alliance of Greek aristocrats, Macedonian kings and Roman viceroys in the succeeding centuries. Greek philosophy is deeply imprinted with these class struggles. The work of the great masters, Socrates, Plato and Aristotle, is in large part a rejection of democracy and an assertion of the exclusive fitness of the elite to rule. Indeed, there is a sense in which Western elite thought ever since can be construed as an attempt to deny democracy in one form or another.[3]

Nevertheless, Greek 'philosophy', unlike modern bourgeois philosophy, was holistic. The word, which is of course Greek, means 'love of knowledge and wisdom' and the Greek philosophers were indeed polymaths, as keen on politics, history and science as on metaphysics. This indulgence involved little risk of any subversive intellectual 'turn'. The audience for their speculations was a safely conservative 'gilded elite', and in any case, no class capable of developing and acting upon a generalised socio-political critique existed.

The same remained true of the Western medieval continuators of the classical tradition of scholarship. Theirs was, if anything, an even more exclusive world than that of their Greek forebears, for medieval scholarship was conducted almost entirely within the Church and using the medium of Latin. It was also holistic, admittedly within the rigid constraints imposed by received text and doctrine, but none the less constituting, or at least purporting to be, a comprehensive world view.

A central feature of the bourgeois revolution growing inside the old order was the way in which this tradition – of an exclusive intellectual elite seeking general knowledge of the world as a whole – burst its clerical shell. The Renaissance and the Enlightenment represented, at one level, the appropriation by lay intellectuals of knowledge stores, methods of scholarship, and analytical tools that had previously been monopolised by churchmen. But what matters for this story are not the revolutionary challenges to received wisdom represented by scholars such as Copernicus, Galileo and Leonardo, or by Isaac Newton, Jean Jacques Rousseau and the French *encylopédistes*, but the continuation of a tradition of holistic research by polymathic scholars situated within a socially exclusive community. The western intelligentsia was larger and more socio-culturally diverse in the eighteenth century compared with the twelfth, but it was still an elite embedded within an apparently secure property-owning class.

This world of intellectual security had been shaken by the upheavals of the Reformation, the Dutch Revolution, the French Wars of Religion, Germany's Thirty Years War and the English Revolution. But it had not been shattered. The revolts of peasants and urban masses had either been crushed outright, or contained and channelled within the social framework of the bourgeois revolution. Of critical significance was the absence of an economically concentrated and socially distinct proletariat of propertyless labourers. The popular movements of the sixteenth and seventeenth centuries were invariably dominated by a petty-bourgeoisie of better-off peasants, master-artisans and small traders. These were pre-industrial struggles. Property-owners certainly feared 'the many-headed multitude', but they were not yet intellectually and politically paralysed by this fear.

In this respect, the late eighteenth century was a watershed. The French Revolution ran deeper than its Dutch, English and American precursors and was significant for its exceptional level of popular organisation and mobilisation and the emergence within this powerful revolutionary-democratic movement of an embryonic proletarian-socialist tendency.

This tendency remained imprisoned within the limits of a bourgeois revolution in an essentially pre-industrial society.

But it spawned an enduring French socialist tradition which would, half a century later, influence two radical German intellectuals, Karl Marx and Frederick Engels. And what made it by this time something more than mere utopian aspiration was the rise of a social class being formed by the other half of Eric Hobsbawm's 'dual revolution': the industrial proletariat. Handicraft production trapped the quasi-proletariat of the pre-industrial age in a world whose dominant social horizons were those of the independent artisan and the small workshop. Factory production destroyed the petty-bourgeoisie and sorted people into two, clearly defined, sharply antagonistic social classes: capitalists and workers. Because the emancipation of the working class was inherently a collective and global project, the emergence of this class as an historical actor placed the existence of private property itself in question – for the first time since the earliest development of class society around 3000 BC.

This contradiction underlay the stillbirth of the bourgeois revolutions of 1848. The bourgeoisie feared the threat from below represented by a popular movement in which the proletarian-socialist tendency was significantly stronger than it had been in 1792. Consequently, it shrank from revolutionary leadership, and instead accommodated to the forces of reaction and absolutism. The popular movement, on the other hand, was too ill-formed and ideologically muddled to provide an alternative leadership. Counter-revolution triumphed. The tasks of the bourgeois revolution – national unity, the free market, civil rights, a liberal constitution – were henceforward to be achieved 'from above'. The Italian *Risorgimento*, German Unification and the American Civil War are all, in their different ways, forms of the 'bourgeois revolution from above', accomplished in ways designed to minimise popular self-activity and keep the 'spectre of communism' bottled.

This is the historical context for the development of the contradiction with which we began: that between the general theory and holistic world view implicit in 'universal' education, and the need to disable critical thought in the presence of a class with an interest in abolishing private property and an increasing potential to do so. The bourgeois 'anti-Enlightenment' had several characteristics that bear on the character of university education today:

- a growing fragmentation of knowledge through increasingly refined subject specialization;
- a retreat from holistic, generalising, and contextualising perspectives within individual subject specialisms;
- a growing dichotomy between abstract/generalising theory and operational/vocational knowledge;
- a rationing of access to abstract/generalising theory, especially with the spread of educational provision for the working class;
- the marginalisation, or outright exclusion, of radical critiques and perspectives.

The development of sociology can serve as an example, as it clearly illustrates all these tendencies. It emerged during the nineteenth century as a response to the 'social problem' posed by the rise of organised labour in general and to the political challenge of Marxism in particular.[4] Its very existence as a discipline that studied the contemporary social order largely independently of history, economics, politics and philosophy made it more difficult to grasp the way in which social phenomena were determined by a totality of social relations and processes that was both contradictory and dynamic. Within the small frame offered by sociology, the whole became invisible and the nature of social reality remained a mystery. Critique became specific rather than general, and thus led naturally towards reformist 'solutions' to particular social problems rather than a revolutionary transformation of all social problems. Vocational 'social work' courses constitute an obvious practical expression of this.

Marxism could not be ignored by sociology. Instead, its revolutionary content was destroyed by its dismemberment. Sociology's treatment of Marxism mirrors its treatment of social reality. Society is fragmented into a set of more or less self-contained, self-referential worlds of social experience. A widely used A-Level sociology textbook,[5] for example, organises knowledge of society into the following categories: social stratification; power, politics and the state; poverty; education; work, unemployment and leisure; organisations and bureaucracy; families and households; sex and gender; crime and deviance; religion; methodology; and sociological theory. Within each of these categories, a 'Marxist perspective' is dutifully explained alongside various others. Only it is not explained, because it is of the very essence of Marxism that it is holistic.

Marxism can be defined as the theory and practice of international working-class revolution. It represents the continuation of the holistic approach to understanding social reality that can be traced from Plato's Academy to the eighteenth century *salons*. Its synthesis of German philosophy, British economics and French socialism can be regarded as the supreme intellectual achievement of Enlightenment thought. But its essential insight – that the entire bourgeois social order was the result of contradictory and irrational processes of capital accumulation, class exploitation, and human alienation – involved it in an abrupt and absolute rupture with mainstream scholarship.

For about a century, the revolutionary potential of social theory could usually be contained within the university by simultaneously compartmentalising knowledge into hermetically sealed academic disciplines and limiting access to higher education to social elites. But the expansion of higher education during the Great Boom following the Second World War reconfigured the contradiction. As large numbers of students from relatively ordinary backgrounds entered the university system for the first time, the rigid frameworks constraining knowledge and understanding came under growing pressure. The international student revolt centred on 1968 was multifaceted, but not least were protests against academic structures and curricula that marginalised radical and generalising social theory. That is why, at the high points of struggle, when campuses were under occupation, mass experiments in creating 'alternative universities' took place. Thousands of young people wanted to debate critical social theories that attempted to explain the world of injustice and violence they found themselves confronting.

The neoliberal counter-revolution of the last generation has involved sustained attempts to block off this kind of educational experimentation, and to reimpose top-down control over schools, colleges, and universities. The comprehensive system, mixed-ability teaching, child-centred learning, multicultural-ism, the freedom for teachers to experiment and innovate – this and much more in our schools has been under attack since the late 1970s. The universities have also changed. The work of academics has become more regulated and pressured. The humanities and the social sciences have been squeezed relative to more 'vocational' subjects. The abolition of maintenance grants and the introduction of fees have both impoverished students and begun the privatisation of the universities. Corporate sponsorship has corrupted the ideal of independent, free-thinking, 'universal' education, skewing curricula towards science, engineering, IT and vocational training. The needs of capital – where the content of education is driven by the demands of the labour market and the international competi-tiveness of British business – have come to predominate over those of both students and society.

'Higher education is fundamental to our national prosperity,' intones the 2010 Labour Party general election manifesto. 'Demand for high-level skills is strong and growing, and the supply of good graduates is an increasingly important factor in global economic competition.'[6] Labour is explicit that in its plan for higher education, 'priority in the expansion of student places will be given to foundation degrees and part-time study, and to science, technology, engineering and mathematics degrees, as well as applied study in key economic growth sectors'.[7] The Tory manifesto is no different. 'Universities contribute enormously to the economy,' it explains in its opening sentence on the subject of higher education.[8] To underline the lesson, it offers a little homily to Silicon Valley, which is described as 'a global beacon for innovation and enterprise' – a success attributed to its 'highly skilled workforce and world-class universities'.[9]

That education is partly about 'how' – about acquiring the knowledge and skills to perform particular productive tasks – is not at issue. Intelligent, collective labour – which depends, of course, on operational knowledge and skill – is a fundamental species characteristic. Social progress, whenever and wherever real social progress occurs, results from the growing accumulation of knowledge and skill that makes labour increasingly productive.

The point at issue is this: 'how' is not enough. We need to know 'why' and 'what'. To know how to make a nuclear missile, a fighter jet or a water cannon does not mean that we necessarily should make them. Of course we need 'vocational' knowledge and skills, but we also need to equip ourselves to ask critical questions, to engage in democratic debate and to make informed choices about social priorities. In this context, 'we' does not include those who currently design our system of university education, for they have little interest in social priorities being collectively and democratically determined.

The expansion of the universities in the 1950s and 1960s created mass higher education for the first time. This in itself created a crisis, even though a large majority of students were still from relatively affluent backgrounds. The further expansion since then has not only quadrupled the number of students : it has also, for the first time, brought large numbers of students from working-class backgrounds onto the campuses. The volatility and explosive potential of modern universities was dramatically revealed by the student revolt of November–December 2010. The drive to privatise, corporatise and 'vocationalise' the universities is not only about turning out skilled labour for British capital. It is also about insulating two million higher-education students from general, critical, holistic, subversive theories of the kind which real universities have an unfortunate tendency to foster. Our rulers are desperate to turn universities into skills factories. The defence of the humanities and the social sciences, as part of the wider struggle against marketisation and instrumentalisation, is a reassertion of the Enlightenment tradition of 'universal' education in the interests of society as a whole and a critical task for the movement today.

NOTES

1. Chris Harman, *The Fire Last Time: 1968 and After* (London: Bookmarks, 1998).
2. Eric Hobsbawm, *The Age of Revolution* (London: Abacus, 1977).
3. Ellen Meiksins Wood, *Citizens to Lords: A Social History of Western Political Thought from Antiquity to the Late Middle Ages* (London: Verso, 2008).
4. Anthony Giddens, *Capitalism and Modern Social Theory* (Cambridge: Cambridge University Press, 1971).
5. Mike Haralambos and Martin Holborn, *Sociology: Themes and Perspectives* (London: Unwin, 1985).
6. Labour Party, *A Future Fair for All*, election manifesto (London: Labour Party, 2010), 3.7.
7. Ibid.
8. Conservative Party, *Invitation to Join the Government of Britain*, election manifesto (London: Conservative Party 2010), p. 17.
9. Ibid.

4

Fighting for the University's Life

Nick Couldry

The UK coalition government's funding reforms are a sustained attack on the idea of the university in England. Unless defended, that idea will die.[1]

Can ideas die? Yes they can: not absolutely, but in particular places, as the paths of thought that enact them in practice become blocked. Whatever its broader ancestry, the idea of the university in England represents the shared commitment of a medium-sized population that practical access to the widest range of human knowledge and creativity should not be restricted by social class or family wealth. The lives of vast numbers of people have been changed by the institutional forms that principle took over the past half-century.

Ironically, the coalition government talks about access too, while simultaneously ensuring the narrowing, and eventual undermining, of what there is for students to 'access'. In the 'new world' that David Willetts, Minister for Universities, invokes,[2] a market of new providers will spring up to offer the skills school-leavers need more efficiently than some of our existing universities, and student-consumers will be empowered to shop around for the best deals. Meanwhile, something larger will have been withdrawn: the government's commitment to fund the infrastructure that made the idea of the university in England a practical reality.

I write not as an expert on the idea or history of the university, but instead as a person whose life chances were transformed by the experience of going to university. At stake is not just a particular set of institutions, but a whole generation's sense of their future.

THE NEOLIBERAL WOLF IN BROWNE'S CLOTHING

The Browne report, published in October 2010,[3] recommended two fundamental things: first, the lifting of the undergraduate fees cap (subsequently reinstated by the government, but at the price of a likely doubling and potential tripling of fees for most students) and second, the withdrawal of governmental teaching support for all courses except 'priority' courses (medical, some other sciences, and 'strategically important language courses'). It is the second proposal that makes the first essential, so it is the second reform on which we should concentrate our analysis.

The actual language of the Browne report has been rather neglected in the public debate so far. The Browne report talks not of cuts or of downsizing the university, but of 'a sustainable funding solution for the future'. The report's first principle is that 'there should be more investment in higher education'. The mechanism to achieve this sounds encouraging too: 'institutions will have to convince students of the benefits of investing more'. 'We want', Browne says, 'to put students at the heart of the system. Students are best placed to make the judgement about what they want to get from participating in higher education.' Even better, 'choice is in the hands of the students' … 'the money will follow the student'.

The gap between the reality of funding cuts and Browne's language of expansion may seem strange. But the gap is precisely the point. What bridges the gap is the underlying principle that the report leaves unspoken: the principle of market liberalism which takes its most radical form in the work of the US economist Milton Friedman.[4] Friedman applied Adam Smith's principle of the 'invisible hand of the market' to argue for a drastic shrinking of government. According to Friedman, the only way that good *social* ends can be achieved is to leave individuals to compete through markets to get what they *individually* want. According to a similar logic, Browne suggests that, with the exception of those degree courses that the government decides are a priority for subsidy, the best way to get improved quality of university teaching is through the choices each *individual* makes in deciding where to apply for university.

On the face of it, the idea that by exercising our freedom of choice as individuals we also get what we want as a society – a higher-quality education system – is attractive, a win–win situation! But it is a myth, the myth of all market liberalism: that the operation of individual choice in market competition is the best or even the only way to achieve social ends. Here in full is the report's 'first principle':

Our proposals introduce more investment for higher education. HEIs must persuade students that they should 'pay more' in order to 'get more'. That money will follow the student.

Pay more? What Browne means is draw down more from money students haven't yet got, based on their expectations of the money they will earn in the future. As a result the courses that will be financially viable in the future will be the courses that student 'purchasers' think are most likely to generate for them higher earnings after they leave. That means (although Browne never says this) that the choice of courses available to students in ten years' time, say, will be determined by the choices of those in five years' time, based principally on their expectations of what level of pay a prospective degree will secure for them.

This tying of the funding of future degree provision to a very narrow model of educational choice is no accident. For Browne argues directly that 'there needs to be a closer fit between what is taught in higher education and the skills needed in the economy'. Priority degrees for government subsidy are those where 'skills and knowledge' are 'currently in shortage or predicted to be in the future': we are talking here exclusively about the needs of the economy. An open educational market will ensure, according to Browne, that economic needs should be the main driver. The long-term outcome is clear: 'courses that deliver improved employability will prosper: those that make false promises will disappear'.

But what about *Browne's* promises? What are we to make of a reform that apparently will lead to better and fairer funding of the English university system but in fact institutes a *pure market* mechanism that will completely transform the principles on which the English higher education system is built? The Browne report – commissioned by the New Labour government – moves decisively away from the principle that governments should support universities to provide access at the highest level to the full range of human knowledge, understanding and creativity and so ensure that young people have the opportunity to develop their full intellectual and creative potential, regardless of family wealth. In its place comes a much cruder principle that the only university functions government supports are those that meet the immediate needs of the economy, and a very narrowly defined definition of 'priority sectors' at that!

However, the violence of this policy shift has hardly been discussed in the mainstream media. Nor is being effectively challenged by the Labour Party, the party that stands to gain most by exploiting the difficulties of the coalition on this point: a rare exception was a short *Guardian* article by John Denham that in late November acknowledged that 'parliament is being rushed into a profound change that threatens the very idea of public universities, publicly funded'.[5]

The reason for this relative silence from mainstream political voices is, I suggest, the reason why neoliberal reforms have typically made progress in Britain unopposed: namely, the reluctance of people, *particularly* on the 'left' (the New Labour project being a classic case study of this reluctance),[6] to articulate values in public which reject the primacy of the market as the sole principle of social and political organisation. Browne believes that a system for distributing resources based on individual market choice will generate the university system that society needs: classic Milton Friedman, even if not classic Friedrich von Hayek (Hayek, less recklessly than Friedman, insisted that markets could *not* satisfy key infrastructural needs such as the road system).[7] The result, as George Monbiot pointed out on the wider cuts,[8] is a subterfuge that is typical of what Naomi Klein calls the 'shock doctrine': imposing radical free-market reforms under the pretext that disaster of some sort requires them – here the threat from looming government debt. As Milton Friedman said three months after the Katrina disaster in 2004 but thinking about the disaster's implications for the provision of public schools in New Orleans: 'this is a tragedy: It is also an opportunity to radically reform the educational system'.[9] Now here on the ground in Britain we are starting to understand what he meant.

But we will not make much progress in confronting this policy violence unless we face explicitly the paradox we have been living in Britain for more than a decade now: neoliberal democracy is more than a misfortune, it is an oxymoron.[10] It is the basic *values* that animate (or fail to animate) our current politics – the regular installing of market values in priority over all other values – that underlie the current crisis of democracy in Britain, and so the impending crisis of the university too.

The very fact that such bold reforms of our higher education system could be attempted under cover of *equalising* access to high education (*don't* read Nick Clegg's lips is surely the motto) is a symptom of a deeper crisis whereby neoliberal democracy consistently *offers* voice, participation, inclusion, but then retracts it. Indeed, the prediction of the leading theorist of the market-state makes a good epitaph to the hopes of many on the left just after the coalition's rise to power in May 2010: 'there will be more public participation in government, but it will count for less'.[11]

COUNTER-CULTURAL VALUES

So there is more at stake in this debate than the future of the university: the marketisation of the university is only one way in which neoliberal reforms in Britain are being accelerated. Wider alliances with those affected by other dimensions of this process are essential. But let me stick to the specific challenge to the life of the university.

Let's be honest. This challenge is hardly unexpected, even if its full force was not anticipated.[12] As UK academics, we have for 15 years been facing – or perhaps *not* facing – the consistent deformation of academic values through the production-line model of research under the RAE and now the Research Excellence Framework (REF). The REF, as English academics were debating only recently (during a consultation on the REF proposals), represents a huge challenge to autonomous academic values, installing 'impact' as a lead criterion of research that has value. The *point* of the REF is to remove core research funding from 'research units' whose research lacks demonstrable impact (that is, 'impact' defined primarily by reference to the economy and policy-making).[13]

So it is hardly surprising that core *teaching* funding is now to be withdrawn from institutions except where they teach in certain priority areas: priorities not for society, but for the national economy, in other words economic sectors where jobs cannot be filled. As in the wider debate on neoliberalism, no one is arguing such areas do *not* need support: the issue is whether they should be supported at the cost of every other type of degree, whether it is design, philosophy, history, most languages, culture, arts, social sciences, literature, and so on.

In the university, as elsewhere, neoliberal doctrine works by being installed as an implacable 'rationality': a force not felt as 'force', but simply as the way particular 'things' now have to be, because of the underlying way that other 'things' are. As Wendy Brown has argued, the only starting-point for resisting neoliberalism is to build explicitly, deliberately, a 'counter-rationality – a different figuration of human beings, citizenship, economic life, and the political'.[14] That counter-rationality must be cunning in bringing out the contradictions within neoliberalism itself. There is not only the incoherence of believing that markets always self-correct (no one can publicly affirm that now, although Lord Browne, as we have seen, implicitly tries), but the *deeper* incoherence that provides cover for neoliberalism's official slogans at the level of 'rationality' and its seemingly uncontroversial values: the 'value' that dictates economic ends take priority over ends, whether social political or cultural; and the 'value' that economic ends alone can be determined autonomously by reference to the sphere of the economy, without reference to other potential ends of the economy.

Although neoliberalism produces incoherences in democratic functioning, in social policy and so on, it *works* because neoliberalism is also a culture: a deeply embedded set of recipes and rules of thumb that have *become* 'the ways things are'.[15] Neoliberal culture then can be opposed only by a strategy that *first* names those incoherences explicitly and *second* offers alternative values which might provide an alternative type of everyday institutional culture.

On the first point, we do have the resources to name the deeper incoherences of neoliberalism: for me, the most valuable tools come from Michel Foucault's lectures on neoliberalism,[16] and, most useful of all, Amartya Sen's critiques of the thin account of freedom and rationality that neoliberal doctrine (which claims to promote those two values) actually provides. One of Sen's forebears is the very same Adam Smith whom neoliberalism, even in its most popular versions, claims as its talisman.

Sen, in his 1987 book *On Ethics and Economics*, argues that economics lost its way when, shortly after Adam Smith, it forgot its connection with ethics – that is, with reflections on the ethical ends, the account of the good life, that economic production should serve. For the ethics that economics needs: 'cannot stop the evaluation [of economic activity] short at some arbitrary point like satisfying "efficiency". The assessment has to be more fully ethical, and take a broader view of the good.'[17] And as Sen wrote in his later book *Freedom and Rationality*, a notion of freedom (such as Lord Browne's) that is reduced to the chance to compete freely in a market tells us nothing about what we are *free for*. For Sen, by contrast, freedom is 'the actual ability of [a] person to achieve those things that she *has reason* to value'.[18] This opens up, from another angle, the social, political, cultural and material (i.e. 'economic') ends of economic production. Sen, from deep within economics, insists that we ask: productivity for what? Efficiency for what? Impact for what?

Re-asking those questions is perhaps the start of resisting the deep embedding of neoliberal culture. But it is clearly not enough, because neoliberalism has ready-made answers to all those questions. So alternative *answers* are needed. Here, in seeking out new starting points for defining the positive values that would animate a counter-rationality to neoliberalism, we need open debate. There will probably be no initial agreement, even among the contributors to this book, on starting points. I would argue for Sen's wider theory of justice and freedom and

German social theorist Axel Honneth's work on recognition. But of course I don't want to conclude by selling you some particular set of values.

Instead my conclusion is more general. We know that external forces (and some internal forces too) are now seeking to close down a university culture where debate about value – discussion that foregrounds what Sen calls 'our values *about* values' – can go on. The best response (perhaps obvious, but the obvious needs saying in the face of a neoliberal culture that grows by not allowing certain types of 'obvious' to be said) is to build a counter-culture within the English university, a culture and a life which embeds a counter-rationality to neoliberalism.

To invoke the 1960s term 'counter-culture' risks being accused of nostalgia. Clearly today's starting points are very different. The counter-culture of the 1960s could rely on the intellectual authority (in Britain, France and the USA, for example) of a smaller, more elitist university system on the brink of historic expansion. Now we face in England drastic university reforms as a prelude to likely contraction whose basic logic *assumes the diminished* authority and relevance of university culture. This, then, is another reason why the struggle for the English university must connect with movements outside the university: arguments for a socially inclusive university must be renewed and reinvigorated so they reconnect with the wider range of citizens, just as repairing the legitimacy of political decision-making requires the political participation of a new range of actors. A critical and reinvigorated vision of the social purpose of university teaching as a tool for expanding and sustaining public knowledge is at the heart of this struggle.[19]

The struggle for the university is a struggle for people's futures, and the role of universities as reference points for hope. The coalition government gambled that those who have already benefited from the university as an institution, and those who still want to, will fail to turn their lived experience, or cherished hope, of transforming their future into present political action. It is important that this gamble is proved wrong.

NOTES

1. See also Nick Couldry and Angela McRobbie, 'The death of the university, English style', *Culture Machine*, 11 November 2010. Available at: http://www.culturemachine.net/index.php/cm/article/view/417/430 [accessed 18 February 2011].

2. Quoted *Guardian*, 26 November 2010.

3. Lord Browne (chairman), *Securing a Sustainable Future for Higher Education*, 12 October 2010. Available at: www.independent.gov.uk/browne-report [accessed 18 February 2011].

4. Milton Friedman, *Capitalism and Freedom*, 2nd edn (Chicago: Chicago University Press, 1982).

5. John Denham, 'Willetts' great fees gamble', *Guardian*, 25 November 2010.

6. See Nick Couldry, *Why Voice Matters: Culture and Politics After Neoliberalism* (London: Sage, 2010), Chapter 3 for discussion.

7. Compare Friedrich von Hayek, *Individualism and Economic Order* (London: Routledge and Kegan Paul, 1949), pp. 107–118 with Friedman, *Capitalism and Freedom*, p. 2.

8. George Monbiot, 'For the Tories this is not a financial crisis but a long-awaited opportunity', *Guardian*, 19 October 2010.

9. Quoted in Naomi Klein, *The Shock Doctrine* (Harmondsworth: Penguin Allen Lane, 2007), pp. 4–5.

10. For a more detailed, argument, see Couldry, *Why Voice Matters*, Chapter 3.

11. Philip Bobbitt, *The Shield of Achilles* (Harmondsworth: Penguin, 2003), p. 234.

12. Note that in a remarkable article Anthony Grafton, arguably the world's leading scholar in historiography, already saw the crisis coming in a piece published in March 2010: Anthony Grafton, 'Britain: The Disgrace of the Universities', *New York Review of Books*, 10 March 2010, p. 32.

13. For more detail, see Nick Couldry, 'Post-neoliberal academic values: notes from the UK higher education sector' in Barbie Zelizer (ed.), *Making the University Matter* (London: Routledge), forthcoming, discussing the New Labour government's 2009 White Paper, *Higher Ambitions: The Future of Universities in a Knowledge Economy*.

14. Wendy Brown, 'Neo-liberalism and the end of liberal democracy', *Theory & Event* 7 (1) (2003), 1–23, para. 42.

15. See especially Henry Giroux, *The Terror of Neoliberalism* (Boulder, CO: Paradigm Books, 2004).

16. Michael Foucault, *Security, Territory, Population: Lectures at the College de France, 1977–78* (Basingstoke: Palgrave Macmillan, 2007).

17. Amartya Sen, *On Ethics and Economics* (Oxford: Blackwell, 1987), p. 4.

18. Amartya Sen, *Rationality and Freedom* (Cambridge, MA: Harvard University Press, 2002), p. 5.

19. See Henry Giroux's lifelong work on 'critical pedagogy' and Edward Said's last book, *Humanism and Democratic Criticism* (Basingstoke: Palgrave, 2004).

Part II

Current Challenges and Future Visions

5

Economic Alternatives in the Current Crisis[1]

Aeron Davis

CONDEM AND FINANCIER ECONOMIC NARRATIVES ... AND OTHER FAIRYTALES

In May 2010 the new Conservative-dominated coalition government came into power with a strong story. It went like this. Under New Labour, the public sector grew far too much. The UK had a bloated, over-bureaucratic state and was now running up unprecedented debts. There was a large annual deficit of 11 per cent of GDP (gross domestic product) and the nation's long-term debt had soared to 66 per cent of GDP in just a couple of years. Their response to the economic downturn was to pump money round the economy, thus creating even more debt. This was unsustainable. Those international investors, who serviced our debts by buying up government gilts (bonds), would not put up with it for much longer. We would go the way of Greece, Ireland and many others before them. The interest rates applied to UK debt would soar, international business would stop investing, and the economy would collapse. So the government made a series of difficult but necessary decisions. The annual deficit had to be cut quickly by cutting public expenditure in every sector. Extra layers of bureaucracy, non-jobs and non-essential services could all be cut easily. Tina (there is no alternative) was paraded in public whenever possible. So was her good friend Waitt (we're all in this together) and her fairy godmother BS (big society). In these circumstances, the HE sector was an easy target: a non-essential public expense producing too many graduates with non-vocational qualifications.

For the next six months this narrative went largely unchallenged. International economic institutions voiced their approval of the plans. The UK retained its AAA credit rating. The Labour Party ('old' or 'new') was occupied by an extended leadership election and a post Blair–Brown identity crisis. Journalists, from left and right, enjoyed their extended summer holidays, and then gave the new government the traditional extended honeymoon period in which to settle in. The leaders of local councils and professional bodies across the nation were slow to respond. Far too many were either dazzled by Tina and the Cameron–Clegg bromance, or steamrollered and threatened with greater cuts if they failed to comply. Most of the cuts, and the reactionary policies linked to them, were not debated in Parliament as they were contained in government budgets rather than legislation. By early 2011 the narrative was more open to criticism but, by then, so much had already been pushed through. The marketisation of HE was a done deal.

For many critical observers this narrative seems fairly Orwellian in its erasing of recent history. It's a bit like that part in 1984 when Oceana and Eastasia, formerly allies at war with Eurasia, are suddenly themselves at war as if they always had been. In this case, where before it was the banks who were to blame for the economic crisis, now it was nation-states, weak regulators and greedy consumers who had maxed out their credit cards. The huge debts of the private banking system were suddenly turned into public sovereign debt. Students, amongst other groups, were going to pay the price while bankers walked off with their huge fortunes.

However, in many ways, it was the radical thinking of 2008–10 that was out of step with the larger narratives and socio-economic policies of the previous three decades. These had begun in the Thatcher–Reagan era and have been maintained regardless of the party in power ever since. These decreed several things that were fundamental to the emerging forms of turbo-charged, globalised and financialised capitalism. Keynesian welfare state policies and overly strong unions had smothered the development of advanced economies. Traditional industries were doomed as developing economies, with much lower labour costs, could make things more cheaply. The ways forward, apart from 'reforming' public services and shackling unions, were to expand on perceived strengths. These lay in raising graduate numbers, developing new technologies, an expansion of the service, IT and financial sectors. There was also a need to attract international investment and 'top talent' by cutting red tape, introducing flexible labour markets and increasing financial incentives (reducing corporate and top levels of tax). Political leaders, while disagreeing on the small print, all pursued these same larger policies. Such beliefs and intentions are as clearly set out in Tony Blair's recent autobiography[2] as they are in (auto) biographies of Margaret Thatcher.

And, indeed, such policies seemed to be working. Global trade increased. Food and clothing got cheaper. Steady growth and employment levels remained fairly stable, give or take the odd bout of 'over-exuberance'. Financial sectors boomed, contributing to rising tax revenues, employment and trade surpluses. In the UK, by 2000, the City employed an estimated 300,000 people, saw an average growth of 7 per cent per year over 25 years, and had an overseas trade surplus of £31 billion.[3] Financial services, bio-tech and hi-tech companies took their place in the higher echelons of stock markets alongside energy companies, supermarkets and traditional industries. So, once the immediate banking crisis had been averted, it seemed appropriate to go back to plan A. That is what was working before and what would also propel the 'new economies' out of their slumps and back to growth and prosperity.

Orwellian sleights of hand apart, there are many bits of truth in these narratives. In the period of New Labour, government spending, as a proportion of GDP, did go up. Bureaucracies got larger, too large and overbearing in many cases. Personal debt levels got too high. Spending in health, higher education and other parts of the welfare state rose. The HE sector flourished as part of this, and undergraduate numbers went up hugely. This itself suggested that the existing funding scheme would have to change to accommodate this rise and, in turn, that the dominant narratives were likely to dictate the form of that change.

However, many bits of these narratives are not true. Some are plain false, purely conjured up by skilled politically and financially elite story-tellers for reasons of political expediency. Others are partial and selective accounts of recent history, chosen because they fit a larger world view.

UNCOVERING THE MISSING NARRATIVES
... THE MINISTRY OF TRUTH UNVEILED

One misleading narrative regards the size of the state. It is often shown that public expenditure as a proportion of GDP has gone up steadily over the last century. In 1900 it was roughly 14 per cent and by 2010 it was 45 per cent. In 1997, when New Labour took over, it was just over 38 per cent. The implication is that the state has grown too large, and that left-leaning governments expand public spending too much. However, this line of argument obscures three significant issues. First, the figure has fluctuated between 38 and 45 per cent across all governments since 1948 (it was over 70 per cent in 1945). Second, this headline figure hides the fact that an increasing proportion of public expenditure has been contracted out to the private sector. The money is collected by the state, but much more of it is now managed outside it. Third, and probably most importantly, is the focus on GDP and government expenditure as measures of state control over the economy. This avoids the key issue of the rise of finance and the control of capital by international financial centres.

In 1979/80, the equity value of the London stock market was roughly 40 per cent of government expenditure. By 1996/97, its value had risen to more than three and a half times government expenditure. In 2007, before the crisis began, the total managed annual expenditure of the UK government was £587 billion and GDP was £1.24 trillion. But the top UK fund managers in the City managed £3.4 trillion. Currency trading had reached $3 trillion a day. The international banking system operated funds of $512 trillion or ten times the GDP value of the entire world economy, or over four hundred times the UK's GDP.[4] Over the last three decades, fairly small groups of international financiers have come to have a huge influence over national economies. Their decisions now significantly affect our banking systems, commodities prices, interest rates, currency values, and so on.

It was indeed the financial sector that dragged national economies into the crisis. Banks and other financial organisations had grown 'too big to fail' and had too much influence over state regulators and governments. There had been several waves of deregulation since the 1980s, in the USA, UK and elsewhere. Successive governments of left and right supported these for the reasons laid out above. By the time of the collapse, the regulated banking system in the USA accounted for some $12 trillion of funds, but the unregulated, or shadow, banking system was worth $16 trillion.[5] Banks and financial institutions could borrow whatever they liked from this unseen black market. They also ended up lending this money on to whoever would borrow it, from poor home-owners to reckless banks and over-ambitious (some might say 'dishonest') political administrations. The other part of the problem was investment banks and other institutions inventing complex financial products that most people, including bankers and regulators, did not understand. These dressed up very risky things, such as sub-prime mortgages, repackaged them to look like low-risk investments, and sold them onto sucker institutions that did not know any better. Another thing was the sudden growth of derivatives markets, which were also subjected to clever financial engineering. By 2008, in just the space of a decade, the total derivatives market rose in value from $15 trillion to $600 trillion, or ten times total world GDP;[6] that is to say, virtual paper values no longer related to real world values. The same could be said of stock markets and property markets.

In effect, financial institutions were just inventing money through complex pyramid or ponzi-style schemes. And out of that invented money and huge profits they paid their top performers – their top fraudsters, you might say – huge salaries and bonuses. But, at some point, those on the inside realised that the figures did not add up. They stopped buying and borrowing, and started calling in the IOUs. The schemes collapsed. Everyone realised there were huge financial black holes. No one knew who owed whom what, or whether all these IOUs had any value. The sclerosis of the virtual financial economy started to hit the real economy. Governments were forced to step in because everyone relied on conventional banking and finance, and that was now completely intertwined with this mass of made-up money, sub-prime mortgages, derivatives, and so on. They had no choice but to intervene.

The combination of shoring up the financial system and combating the sudden economic downturn was what turned a relatively small annual UK deficit and national debt level into something more serious. In 2007 the UK's debt was 22 per cent of its GDP. This was rather lower then it had been in 1997 and was far less than many advanced economies including those of Germany, Japan, France, Italy and the USA. The debt level tripled in two years, although is still lower than those same countries. Between 2007 and 2009 the UK government spent £289 billion to bailout its banks,[7] effectively nationalising many of them. Debt levels also shot up because the economy was in sudden decline and unemployment levels were rising rapidly. This meant that tax revenues dropped and welfare claims rose. A series of fiscal stimulus packages, from quantitative easing to infrastructure projects, contributed further. In other words, until 2007, UK debt levels were not deemed to be a real problem.

The response of the new Conservative-dominated government has been to cut the deficit faster and in larger amounts than most other indebted nations. But the cuts are also cover for grander schemes related to the longer-term dominant narratives and ideology described above. The simplistic belief is that the private sector will step in to replace the shrinking public sector and will do the same things, only more cheaply and more efficiently. There is also the belief that the UK must remain attractive to international corporations and investors, and that the financial sector is still a strong industry that can help the UK recover. So corporation tax is being lowered from 28 per cent to 24 per cent, the top rate of income tax is still only 50 per cent, and special bank taxes are being reduced overall. Back in 1979, corporation tax was 52 per cent and the top rate of income tax was 83 per cent. Bankers' pay and bonus levels remain absurdly high. The government has done little in the way of substantive structural reform to the financial sector and, in fact, is introducing further tax loopholes to entice those with money to invest.

The public are told a different story: Tina, Waitt and BS. The cuts and restructuring are presented as being about increasing 'local choice', 'fairness', 'opportunity' and 'autonomy' for professionals and citizens. But it is marketisation and privatisation and the erosion of equality and local autonomy. We are told that the pain is being shared equally. But it is now clear that bankers and big earners are being taxed less. VAT, the tax that affects those on low incomes most, is the one tax rising. The harshest cuts have been to poorer, mostly Labour-run local councils and to those on benefits. The voluntary sector is being starved of resources. The EMA (Education Maintenance Award), which encourages poor students to remain in education, is being abandoned. In such a climate, university education has been seen as an easy and justified target. Cutting the entire teaching budgets for courses that do not make an obvious market contribution, and forcing students to pay for their courses, can only make HE more 'productive' for the economy. But, again, it is presented as 'student choice' and making UK universities internationally competitive. The government are adamant that the loans given to students to study will not be 'debt'. We are back to Orwellian 'double speak' again.

The government can find many voices of approval for its economic plans. These have tended to dominate news coverage and public debate. However, there are a whole host of critical economists and commentators who think otherwise. Paul Krugman, Joseph Stiglitz and Christopher Pissarides, all Nobel prize-winning economists, each argue that government policy will only make things far worse. Unemployment will rise, spending will slow, and deficits will grow. This is what happened in the 1930s and to many economies around the world since, following the imposition of dramatic cuts programmes. It has been happening in Ireland for the last year. Others, such as Will Hutton and the Centre for Research on Socio-Cultural Change (CRESC), have argued for years that the UK financial sector has long hindered the growth of the real UK economy.

Far too high a share of corporate profits does not get reinvested in research and investment and, instead, becomes accumulated by the super-rich and/or used to gamble on financial markets around the world. No one believes the private sector will simply step in and provide employment, real investment and growth to fill the gap. Instead these authors argue that further funding for research and education, not cuts, is a strong stimulus to growth, and this is exactly what many rival economies are now doing.

At best, the government has a blind faith in the power of markets, big business and the financial services industry. Somehow they, along with the 'Big Society' will magically fix everything. At worst the UK political and economic system appears to have been entirely corrupted. There are 23 millionaires in the Cabinet. One hundred and thirty-four Conservative MPs and Peers were (or still are) employed in the financial sector. In recent years that same financial sector has provided 50 per cent of the party's funds.[8]

THERE ARE ALTERNATIVES … FAREWELL TINA, WAITT AND BS

If the prevailing narratives and crude market ideology that have dominated in recent decades are questioned properly then, of course, there are alternatives. First, cuts do not have to be made as sweepingly or as quickly. Government spending does not simply amount to further debt but, in many cases, stimulates employment, demand and growth. Second, there is huge scope to raise taxes. Raising the top rates of income tax and banking taxes, and introducing higher rates for large bonuses and the super-rich, are all justified and will have far less impact on personal spending than the VAT rise. Third, estimates from the Treasury and PCS Union put tax avoidance and tax evasion costs somewhere between £97 and 150 billion annually,[9] equivalent to the annual deficit alone. Much could be done here. Fourth, there are real choices about what things in society should be cut. Defence cuts were very small compared to those in higher education or welfare. Why should the UK still spend many billions annually fighting wars abroad rather than spend that money on health, welfare and education? Fifth, there could be a real reversal of industrial and economic policy which has favoured financial services over investment in education, research and industry. New banking and lending structures could be created to encourage small and medium-sized businesses. These latter investments are more likely to increase real employment, equality and exports, rather than further contributing to the pockets of the super-rich. In other words, there is no need to privatise the university sector and other parts of the welfare state under the cover of necessary cuts.

NOTES

1. The following sources all provide clear critiques of the UK's economic policies in recent years, the current government's cuts agenda, and the part played by the City. They also offer several alternatives: L. Elliott and D. Atkinson, *The Gods that Failed: How the Financial Elite Have Gambled Away Our Futures* (London: Vintage, 2009); W. Hutton, *Them and Us: Changing Britain – Why We Need a Fair Society* (Little, Brown, 2010); P. Krugman, *The Return of Depression Economics and the Crisis of 2008* (London: Penguin Books, 2008); R. Wilkinson and Pickett, *The Spirit Level: Why Equality is Better for Everyone* (London: Penguin, 2009); False Economy at: http://falseeconomy.org.uk

2. T. Blair, *A Journey* (London, Hutchinson: 2010).

3. T. Golding, *The City: Inside the Great Expectations Machine* (London: FT/Prentice Hall, 2004), p. 10.

4. A. Davis 'The Mediation of Finance' in D. Winseck and D. Jin (eds), *Media Political Economies: Hierarchies, Markets and Finance in the Global Media Industries* (London: Bloomsbury, 2011).

5. UNCTAD, *The Global Economic Crisis: Systemic Failures and Multilateral Remedies, UNCTAD/GDS/2009/1* (New York/Geneva: United Nations Conference on Trade and Development, 2009), p. 13.

6. V. Cable, *The Storm: The World Economic Crisis and What it Means* (London: Atlantic Books, 2009), p. 34.

7. CRESC, *An Alternative Report on UK Banking Reform: A Public Interest Report from CRESC* (Manchester: Centre for Research on Socio-Cultural Change, 2009).

8. See Robert Peston blog at: http://www.bbc.co.uk/blogs/thereporters/robertpeston [accessed 9 February 2011].

9. See Public and Commercial Services Union (2010) 'There is an Alternative': http://www.pcs.org.uk/

6
Re-Imagining the Public Good

Jon Nixon

Throw the forbidden places open
Let the dragons and the lions play.
E.P. Thompson[1]

Having entered Tiananmen Square by way of Qianmen Gate you will see ahead of you the Chairman Mau Memorial Hall and beyond that the Monument to the People's Heroes. To the left you will see the Great Hall of the People and to the right the National Museum of China. As you walk past the Monument to the People's Heroes you will see ahead of you the Gate of Heavenly Peace leading to The Forbidden City. You will enter the forecourt, join the queue, pay the fee, pass the security cordon, and enter through the Meridian Gate into the outer precincts of the Forbidden City. Beyond you are the Hall of Middle Harmony, the Hall of Preserving Harmony, the Hall of Supreme Harmony, and, finally, the Imperial Garden. Along the way you will have been closely observed by innumerable security guards, security police and other less visible agents of the state. You will also have been watched over by innumerable carved dragons at play and the stone lions forever protective of the forbidden places.

THE PUBLIC GOOD

Economists promote a neat definition of 'the public good': products or services of which anyone can consume as much as desired without reducing the amount available for others. Multiple individuals can consume such products or services without diminishing their value, and an individual cannot be prevented from consuming them whether or not the individual pays for them. These text book distinctions hinge on what are referred to as the 'non-rivalry' and 'non-excludability' criteria: public goods are 'non-rivalrous' and 'non-excludable' in the sense that they are accessible to all (without my consumption reducing your consumption) and 'non-excludable' in the sense that we all have access to them (regardless of our ability to pay for the air we breathe).

These over-tidy distinctions – relating to what is and is not designated 'a public good' – mask the ethical and political issues that are at stake. Goods are not of themselves either public or private. Their designation as one or the other is a matter of history or more precisely how people choose to make for themselves a history – what they choose to throw open. A private good becomes a public good only through a process whereby the public gains ownership of what was previously under private ownership. Similarly, a public good becomes a private good only through a process whereby the public loses ownership of what was previously under public ownership. In either case that process constitutes the core of democratic politics: the struggle to define who owns what.

Within that process of struggle the notion of 'the public' – what constitutes 'the public' – is itself highly contested. Within an unrestrained monarchy 'the public' may be little more than a body of office holders dependent on the Crown for status and courtly prestige. Central to the republican ideal is the idea of 'the public' as an expanded 'body politic' of republican citizens endowed with political will and purpose. Within the modern post-republican state 'the public' is literate and reasonable, critical in the defence and promotion of its own vested interests, external to the direct exercise of political power, and deeply committed to the ideal of individual freedom. It comprises a more or less informed electorate. This 'modern' construction of 'the public' is, as Dan Hind puts it, a 'public of private interests' that has produced 'the paradox of modern power, the fact of a secret public'.[2]

THE PRIVATISED PUBLIC

The 'big society' as envisaged by the current UK coalition government comprises just such a 'public of private interests' that has set itself resolutely against the case for 'big government'.[3] This privatised public remains quietly but determinedly protective of the gross inequalities that support and perpetuate its own vested interests. It is a public without a polity, a polity without a citizenry: a public the economic sustainability of which is based not only on pre-existing levels of inequality, but on escalating inequality. The supposedly classless society is as riddled with inequality as its class-based predecessor: 'at the top', suggests Erik Olin Wright, '[is] an extremely rich capitalist class and corporate managerial class, living at extraordinarily high consumption standards, with relatively weak constraints on their exercise of economic power'; at the bottom is 'a pattern of interaction between race and class in which the working poor and the marginalised population are disproportionately made up of racial minorities'.[4] How we characterise these extremes is open to question and to theoretical speculation. That the gap between the extremes is widening and has been for the past 30 years is an incontrovertible fact.

As Polly Toynbee and David Walker (2009) point out, within the UK the gap between rich and poor is particularly marked: 'the UK was and remains far less equitable than other European Union countries. While the top 10% of income earners get 27.3% of the cake, the bottom 19% get just 2.6%. Twenty years ago the average chief executive of one of the top hundred companies on the FTSE index earned 17 times the average employee's pay. By 2008, the typical FTSE boss earned 75.5 times the average.' Toynbee and Walker estimate that as a group the wealthiest pay less in tax than the tax payers in the lowest income bracket: 'take the 1,000 people who appeared in the *Sunday Times* Rich List for 2007 ... If in 2007 Her Majesty's Revenue and Customs had secured the 10% of their capital gains and 40% of their higher-bracket income as Parliament ordained, the Treasury would have been better off by £12 billion, simply by collecting what is avoided.' [5]

But not even the UK can compete with the USA in the accumulation of inequality. As Tony Judt points out, 'in the US today, the "Gini coefficient" – a measure of the distance separating rich and poor – is comparable to that of China'. The comparison is significant, argues Judt, because it runs counter to the grand narratives of opportunity and aspiration that characterise 'the American dream': 'when we consider that China is a developing country where huge gaps will inevitably open up between the wealthy few and the impoverished many, the fact that here in the US we have a similar inequality coefficient says much about how far we have fallen behind our earlier aspirations'. Insofar as those earlier aspirations pointed towards a more just and equal society – a reduction in the gap between 'the wealthy few and the impoverished many' – then the last three decades undoubtedly mark a collective failure. We have become accustomed to injustice and inequality. 'We have', comments Judt, 'adapted all too well and in consensual silence'.[6]

THE CULT OF PRIVATISATION

What can account for this 'consensual silence'? Judt argues that a large part of the reason is to be found in the process of privatisation: 'in the last thirty years, a cult of privatisation has mesmerized Western (and many non-Western) governments'.[7] Like any cult, the 'cult of privatisation' presents itself as an enlightenment project: an exit route from the dark cave of unknowing. In this case the dark cave is budgetary constraint and privatisation is the exit route. Privatisation appears to save money: 'if the state owns an inefficient public program or an expensive public service – a waterworks, a car factory, a railway – it seeks to offload it onto private buyers.'[8] Not only will the private buyers reduce public expenditure, but they will also manage the expensive public service – the energy utility, the public transport system, and, increasingly, higher education – with (so the argument goes) much more efficiency than their public sector counterparts.

That is the rationale by which 'the public of private interests' justifies the increasing privatisation of higher education and the increasing disparity of institutions across the higher education sector. The older universities have almost permanent and undisputed occupancy of the premier league, the post-1992 universities are well represented across the broad span of second league institutions, and the bottom league is occupied almost entirely by institutions that have gained university status more recently. League tables are a self-fulfilling prophesy whereby those institutions located at the top recruit high-profile academic staff, attract the bulk of available research funding, and select students from a small and highly privileged pool of often privately educated applicants.

In an analysis covering over one million university student admissions during the period 2002–2006, the Sutton Trust documented for the first time the extent to which a few individual schools supply the majority of students to the UK's leading research universities – and with lower academic qualifications.[9] 'Basically put,' as the Chairman of the Sutton Trust remarks in his foreword to the report, 'a student in a state school is as likely to go on to a leading university as a student from the independent sector who gets two grades lower at A+ level'.[10] The social capital – or cache – of the public school entrant outbids the academic achievements of the state school entrant. Private interest – and privilege – win over the common good.

The analysis, based on admissions figures for 3,700 schools with sixth forms, sixth form colleges and further education colleges across the UK during the period from 2002 to 2006, provides disturbing evidence of extreme inequalities across the system. Focusing on a group of 13 leading research-led institutions whose degree courses generally have the most stringent entry requirements, the report confirmed that the feeder schools supplying entrants to these universities are reserved almost exclusively for those children from privileged backgrounds: 'independent schools – representing just 7% of schools and 15% of A-level entrants – dominate the university rankings. These schools are available to those children whose parents can afford fees. The remaining places are taken up by state schools that are themselves socially selective – either as a consequence of academic selection or by being situated in a middle class area.'[11]

Moreover, of these elite feeder schools, those with the highest admission rates to the 13 leading universities are highly socially selective. The top 100 schools are, for example, composed of 83 independent (fee-paying) schools, 16 (state-funded, selective) grammar schools and one (state-funded) comprehensive school, while the top 30 schools are composed of 13 independent (fee-paying) schools, 16 (state-funded, selective) grammar schools and one (state-funded) comprehensive school. Figures relating to student admissions to Cambridge and Oxford Universities present a similarly bleak picture of social selection and systemic inequality. Here the top 100 schools with the highest admission rates are composed of 78 independent (fee-paying) schools, 21 grammar (state-funded, selective) schools, and one (state-funded) comprehensive school, while the top 30 schools are composed of 29 independent (fee-paying) schools and one (state-funded, selective) grammar school – and not a single state-funded comprehensive school in sight.

REPRODUCING INEQUALITY

The inequalities evident in patterns of entry to institutions of higher education as documented above are reflected in the entry patterns to the older professions. The funnel effect whereby the privately educated gain a disproportionate share of places at the leading universities has the further effect of ensuring that they fill not only a disproportionate number of posts within the older professions but also a disproportionate number of top posts within those same professions. The deep codes of chronic structural inequality remain: institutional stratification across the higher education sector, the reproduction of privilege through the selective mechanisms of higher education, and the consolidation of private and professional elites.

Thus, for example, the legal profession is top heavy with those who have been independently educated. Again the Sutton Trust highlights inequalities inherent in and reproduced by the system: 'our findings show that in both samples [1989 and 2004] over two thirds of barristers at the top commercial chambers went to fee-paying schools and over 80 per cent were educated at Oxford or Cambridge, while very few went to universities outside the top 12 – just seven per cent in 2004'.[12] A similar pattern emerges from a 2006 Sutton Trust study of the educational backgrounds of leading journalists: 'over half (54%) of the country's leading news journalists were educated in private schools, which accounts for 7% of the school population as a whole'.[13] To argue that such individuals are appointed on merit is to miss the point: merit in such cases is, in part at least, a consequence of gross inequality.

The elected chamber of the UK Houses of Parliament fares better, with the Sutton Trust reporting that 'almost one third (32%) of current MPs attended independent schools, which educate just 7% of the population'.[14] The Madano Partnership (2009) predicted from its ongoing survey that there would be a marked increase in the proportion of new MPs who were privately educated compared with the last intake in 1997. From their figures they forecast that a third of all new MPs would have been to fee-paying schools, compared with 13 per cent of new arrivals when the House of Commons last underwent major change in 1997.[15] As we now know, 23 of the 29 members of the Coalition cabinet are millionaires.

The UK National Equality Panel has provided further evidence in its independent report (Hills et al, 2010) of the cumulative effect of inequality across the life cycle: 'we see this before children enter school, through the school years, through entry into the labour market, and on to retirement, wealth and resources for retirement, and mortality rates for later life. Economic advantage and disadvantage reinforce themselves across the life cycle, and often on to the next generation.'[16] This cross-generational reproduction of inequality is evident in the pattern of student achievement within higher education: 'two thirds of those with professional parents received firsts or upper seconds, but only half of those with unskilled parents. White students were the most likely to get firsts or upper seconds, and Black and Pakistani/Bangladeshi students the least likely.'[17]

RE-IMAGINING TOGETHER

The authority and legitimacy of any democracy are based upon the will and participation of the people. They cannot be transferred to the vagaries of the market – or patched up with intellectually bankrupt notions such as 'the big society' – without putting at risk democracy itself. (Anyone in the slightest doubt as to the intellectual bankruptcy of 'the big society' idea should read David Cameron's most recent attempt to defend it.[18]) The democratic state exists not – as in the case of the totalitarian state – to impose its own independent will, but to interpret and mediate the will of the citizens that constitute and shape its future direction. They are its constitution. That is why Tony Judt insists that, at this particular ethical and political juncture, we not only have to stop and think, but more specifically to stop and think about the constitution of the state. We must, as he puts it, 'learn to "think the state" once again' – think, that is, the 'collective interests, collective purposes, and collective goods' that constitute the state and without which the state ceases to exist as a viable democratic entity.[19]

But how are we to 'think the state' when the state has disappeared into the thick fog of semi-private, semi-public provision? How are we to locate it? How are we to relate to it? Ministers of state may inform us that the state no longer governs from a single locus of power, but devolves power through networks of governance; yet state control of higher education through admissions and funding policies and through the mechanisms of bureaucratic accountability becomes increasingly invasive. The state seems to veer unpredictably between what central government sees as a strategy of decentralised enablement and what at the institutional level is experienced as a relentlessly disabling policy of centralised control. Torn between rolling itself back and pushing itself forward, the state is increasingly out of joint. Learning to 'think the state' means learning to think the necessary relation between the state and the public.

It means re-imagining higher education as a public good. In a democracy what is good for the state has to be for the good of the polity – and what is good for the polity is for the polity to determine. How, then, might we set about this task of imaginative reclamation? How might we 'throw the forbidden places open'?

1. We might start by acknowledging that higher education is not synonymous with the university. Higher education is conducted in most university settings, but is also conducted in a range of other educational settings: the workplace, further education colleges, public libraries, the home, internet cafes, etc. Throwing the forbidden places open means, among other things, valuing these other places of learning as contributing to the public space of higher education. That is not to devalue the university, but simply to speak back to the assumption that the university has a monopoly on higher education. Universities must reach out, render themselves more permeable and accessible, and re-orient themselves beyond their own institutional interests.

2. More specifically, higher education must re-imagine its institutional connectivity with further education, secondary schooling, primary schooling, and early-years provision. Universities are far too ready to lay the blame for their own inadequacies on the quality of state provision. This is the continuing lament of vice-chancellors and principals of elite universities whose admission figures display an appalling disregard for social equity and the equalising of opportunity and outcome across society. School students, further education students, university students, teachers and lecturers, and parents know this is a big lie. No one in their right democratic mind wants universities to be finishing academies for the privately educated sons and daughters of privileged elites.

3. Higher education must help re-define new forms of civic engagement. The gains of the post-1945 settlement were,

across the UK, of huge democratic importance. But we cannot simply loop back to that earlier social democratic settlement. Nor can we wholly reject it. In moving forward we need a vision of higher education that will help us become resilient and assertive citizens who look to the future for the reconstitution of the public good. Higher education still has to find a voice within this debate on what constitutes citizenship within the twenty-first century. The crucial issue, then, as now, is how to move beyond a meritocratic framework that has manifestly failed to deliver on the basic requirements of a fair and equal society.

4. Finally, the public good now has to be defined with reference to a pluralist world society. The internationalisation of higher education has become so marketised and commercialised that there is a possibility of losing sight of the broader cosmopolitan vision of global governance, cosmopolitan learning and global citizenship. Higher education must be about helping ourselves to live together in a world of incommensurable difference and uncompromising contingency. All occurrences are both local and global and as such have both unforeseen and unforeseeable consequences. The world is not going to stop being like this. On the contrary, it will become increasingly super-complex in its inter-connectivity and will make ever increasing demands on our human capacity to understand.

When the people came to the public places – the streets, the public squares, the parks – they did so *together*. What has been remarkable – and, indeed, historic – about the 2011 student demonstrations in the UK against the three-fold increase in student fees is that university students, students in further education, sixth form students, teachers and lecturers, parents and friends, were side by side. They came to reclaim the public good: to 'throw the forbidden places open'. We are beginning to see – once again – how democracy works, what democracy is about, why democracy is vitally important. We have seen, on the streets of Tunisia, Egypt, Bahrain and Libya, what is at stake and what immense sacrifices the struggle for democracy demands. This is not the first time that we have seen democracy in action. Nor will it be the last. But the polity is speaking back and the public good is re-asserting itself. The dragons and the lions are at play.

NOTES

1. E.P. Thompson, *Collected Poems* (Newcastle Upon Tyne: Bloodaxe Books, 1999), p. 125.
2. Dan Hind, *The Return of the Public* (London and New York: Verso, 2010) p. 44.
3. Jeff Madrick, *The Case for Big Government* (Princeton and Oxford: Princeton University Press, 2009).
4. Erik Olin Wright, 'Understanding class: towards an integrated analytical approach', *New Left Review*, 60, Nov./Dec. 2009, pp. 101–116. See p. 114.
5. Polly Toynbee and David Walker, *Unjust Rewards: Ending the Greed that is Bankrupting Britain* (London: Granta Books, 2009), see pp. 6–7 and p. 18.
6. Tony Judt, 'What is living and what is dead in social democracy?', *The New York Review of Books*, LVI, 20, 17 December 2009–13 January 2010, pp. 86–96. See p. 88.
7. Ibid.
8. Ibid.
9. Sutton Trust, *University Admissions by Individual Schools* (London: The Sutton Trust, 2008).
10. Ibid., p. 1.
11. Ibid., p. 18.
12. Sutton Trust, *Sutton Trust Briefing Note: The Educational Backgrounds of The UKs Top Solicitors, Barristers and Judges* (London: The Sutton Trust, June, 2005), see p. 5.
13. Sutton Trust, *The Educational Background of Leading Journalists* (London: The Sutton Trust, June 2006), see p. 4.
14. Sutton Trust, *The Educational Background of Members of the House of Commons and House of Lords* (London: The Sutton Trust, December, 2005), see p. 2.

15. Madano Partnership, *The Class of 2010* (London: Madano Partnership, 2009).
16. John Hills et al, *An Anatomy of Economic Inequality in the UK: Report of the National Equality Panel*. CASE Report 60 (London: Government Equalities Office/CASE, London School of Economics and Political Science, January 2010), see p. 386.
17. Ibid., p. 366.
18. David Cameron, 'Have no doubt the big society is on its way', *The Guardian*, 12 February 2011.
19. Judt, 'What is living and what is dead in social democracy?', p. 92.

7

The War Against Democracy and Education

Nick Stevenson

The recent formation of the Conservative and Liberal government in the UK context has intensified a war against democracy. This might at first glance be a hard argument to substantiate given the avowedly 'liberal' stance of the administration. However, if we view democracy as a set of complex social and cultural practices that help develop relatively open public spaces then this might lead to a shift in perspective. In seeking to understand democracy we need to contrast what might be called the aggregative and deliberative models. If by democracy we mean a competition between different preferences that allows voters to choose between different parties in relatively open elections there would be little sense in talking of the erosion of democracy. Clearly there are no 'constitutional problems' with the formation of the new government after the inconclusive outcome of the 2010 election. In the aggregative model preferences are simply added up and governments are formed by elected elites. The coalition between the Liberals and Conservatives has consistently claimed in this respect that if they are to govern responsibly this means reducing the size of the public deficit. Even if this means ditching 'promises' made to the public in the course of the campaign they have little choice but effectively to privatise the universities and to downsize the public sector. The problem in democratic terms (and it is this that has sparked the public anger) is this is clearly not what was presented to the public during the election campaign, who in effect voted for parties that had much more cautious deficit reduction plans.

If we change the argument and want to talk about democracy in a different sense then the coalition looks somewhat different. As Iris Marion Young argues, the problem with the aggregative model is that it fails to have anything meaningful to say about the quality of the interlocking publics that are formed and suggests that citizenship is a practice that requires little by the way of participation.[1] The deliberative model, on the other hand, requires citizens to engage in democratic discussions concerning different points of view. This requires the constitution of different kinds of public space where critical perspectives can be formulated, voiced and rethought in light of ongoing discussions. While the deliberative model tends to overstate the importance of rationality it does at least require more from citizens than the simple task of voting and asks us to attend to the quality of democratic debate and discussion. Further, we might add that without a relatively egalitarian society based upon universal rights the state is more likely to respond to the expressed needs of powerful elites than ordinary citizens. Massive inequalities, powerful business elites, weak trade unions and poverty are all bad for democratic involvement. Here I shall argue that the Conservative and Liberal Democrat government (the ConDems) are actively involved in a strategy that is hostile to the expression of meaningful forms of democracy.

Freedom, for Cornelius Castoriadis, is dependent upon the struggle for democratic public spaces where we can decide upon our common affairs.[2] This depends upon traditions of free thinking, speech and questioning that are dependent upon two basic norms of citizenship. The first is that we each have an equality to be able to speak our minds and to express our different views. This, as I have suggested, becomes systematically distorted in a system where wealth and power becomes concentrated into the hands of the few. The second is for citizens to be sincere about what they say and not to attempt to mislead one another in respect of their propositions and proposals. Here we might mention 'promises' to abolish tuition fees, reduce bankers' bonuses, and protect child benefit, the EMA and the NHS, to mention only a few.[3] Neither the Liberals nor the Conservatives were as truthful as they might have been during the election campaign, and they are now involved in a top-down project to reinvent British society. The attack on democracy then has seen the further erosion of social citizenship and an increasing cynicism in respect of the way in which the public is manipulated by debate. This, then, is a war on democracy.

WAR ON DEMOCRACY AND EDUCATION

Ulrich Beck suggested that democracy after the end of the Cold War could no longer be said to have 'enemies'.[4] If the Cold War organised public space as a battle between democracy and totalitarianism this metaphor no longer made sense. The disintegration of the idea of Western and Eastern blocs in the European context ushered in more mobile enemies (Islam, Iraq, ecological protestors, etc.) and attendant stereotypes. Democracy, Beck hoped, could find greater global expression while having less permanent 'enemies'. Additionally, Beck argued that the collapse of communism ushered in the possibility of what he called 'the round-table state'.[5] This idea, like Anthony Giddens's notion of the 'third way',[6] clearly belongs to the period in the British context dominated by the New Labour administration. Here the state should engage in processes that seek what Giddens calls the 'democratising of democracy'.[7] This involves constitutional reform, the expansion of the public sphere, the devolution of power, citizen's juries and more flexible decision-making structures. These features would increase the capacity of civil society to take a more active role in self-government, thus breaking from old-style statist social democracy where the potential of civil society was rendered largely passive. However, the third way had too little to offer the poor other than market discipline, and was mainly concerned to stop the middle classes from opting out of public institutions. Third way information economy arguments did not offer enough reflection on questions of inequality and the radical curtailment of the freedom of those who do not have the educational ability to be able to make use of new sources of information. Indeed, the third way failed to develop radical alternatives to neoliberalism where education was largely dictated by the needs of the economy and relied upon a catalogue of tests, inspections and targets to drive up standards. Despite the emphasis upon the expansion of civil society the third way failed to offer progressive initiatives on either the reform of the media or education.

Previously I have described New Labour's approach to education as the 'X factor doctrine'. Here I argue that there are parallels between a new wave of entrepreneurial programming on British television, the emergence of academy schools and the championing of upward mobility and equal opportunity by New Labour. That is to say, the barriers to upward advancement were to be overcome through the deliberate promotion of entrepreneurialism and the new opportunities being created by the knowledge society. The problem with this approach, however, is that it failed to offer an education that was genuinely devoted to the exploration of different ethical alternatives to a minimal democracy and a politics largely driven by the need for as many people as possible to enjoy lifestyles built upon hyper-consumption. If the 'X factor' was a popular television programme that sought to populise the American dream then the approach to education seemed to offer something similar, namely, upward mobility and 'success' in the labour market. In other words, New Labour failed to build upon the narratives that link democracy and education evident within earlier social democratic perspectives. Instead, its key idea was to expand higher education and drive up standards within schools to help deliver an 'aspirational' society in the belief that this would help reposition Britain as a highly skilled and well-educated competitor in a flexible global market place.

There is, however, little evidence to suggest that the radical expansion of higher education has led to the alteration of the class structure. Even conservative cultural commentators like Ferdinand Mount admit that the decline in deference and class privilege has been considerably overstated.[8] But third way arguments radically underestimate the extent to which a deep ambivalence about democracy is a permanent feature of established elites. And that is why we need to look at how elites have managed to reproduce themselves within the new information economy, but also how they have increasingly sought to restrict the development of democratic practices. Hence my wanting to argue that the narrative that joined together the expansion of educational opportunity and democratisation consistently failed to recognise the ways in which capitalist class societies seek to close down democratic practices. Following the example of Jacques Rancière, I wish to suggest that democracy has a permanent 'enemy' in terms of those who want to restrict its practice beyond established elites.[9] This is why democratic systems need to permanently regulate democracy within certain boundaries. Otherwise ideas of participatory citizenship could lead to a potentially unstoppable growth in democratic and critical conversation breaking into the mainstream.

FROM NEW LABOUR TO THE CONDEMS: A QUESTION OF CITIZENSHIP

The recent changes in policy in education needs to be seen in terms of a continuation with certain elite strategies from the past. The main difference lies in terms of the progressive abandonment of any idea of social citizenship (that was still evident within New Labour) for a more hard-nosed liberal citizenship. The historical sociologist Michael Mann has argued that over the course of the twentieth century a form of social citizenship developed as a means of incorporating capitalism into a state-governed system of welfare.[10] This benefited ruling elites as it detracted from and held in check more naked forms of class conflict. However, there were other strategies that were available to ruling elites, such as the more overtly liberal capitalist model represented by the United States. Here there was less emphasis upon social rights, but more upon the role of charity, the duty to work and private provision more generally. Notably the ConDems have already begun to encourage arts, educational and charity organisations to rely more heavily upon private donors, introduced a much harsher benefits regime (in particular emphasising benefit cheats rather than tax avoidance) and have begun the process of converting universities into private institutions. If New Labour retained a strong historic connection to the idea of social citizenship and the welfare state the same could not be said of the current government. Indeed, the robust application of neoliberalism or free market liberalism takes us to the heart of the political strategy adopted by the coalition.

Liberal capitalist ideologies tend to emphasise personal responsibility, the rule of the market, lower tax rates, the waste of the welfare state, the need to curb the power of trade unions and consumer freedoms. Political parties pursuing these policies tend to increase the level of inequality, privatise wherever they can and support the dominance of corporations. During the 1980s neoliberalism mark 1 (otherwise known as Thatcherism) substantially undermined the role of trade unions and the social state, privatised public utilities, increased levels of inequality and reduced levels of taxation. Neoliberalism mark 2 (pursued by the ConDems) furthers this agenda by bringing new areas of social life into the market place and seeking to reduce the size of the state. For example, the Browne report (the document that has led to the increase in student fees) explicitly seeks to replace a system of higher education regulated in terms of the public good with a market that seeks to respond to student demand.[11] The removal of the block grant in respect of the finance of universities and its replacement with student fees is the most controversial measure being proposed. The idea here is that as students are converted into customers they will demand 'better' services and thereby improve the quality of higher education. Hence David Willetts' argument that the 'universities that offer the best teaching arrangements and facilities – and can demonstrate that their graduates are successful – will themselves be more successful at recruiting applicants'.[12]

This, then, is a market system where those unafraid to lend money to do expensive courses will be part of a system increasingly geared to satisfying consumer demand. However, just as the third way's emphasis upon democracy and civil society sought to mask the extent to which the class structure and capitalism were inhospitable to these ideals, the same could be said of the idea of consumer choice. It is not immediately apparent (as has been widely publicised) why poorer students who tend to be more fearful of debt would run the risk of going to elite high fee-paying universities. Perhaps more to the point is the way in which the languages of markets and choices aims to legitimise a system of higher education where the privileged will still be able to command places at the top universities and where the freedoms of other citizens are massively constrained. The gradual shrinking of social welfare, increasing inequality and encouragement only to think in terms of market advantage is clearly in the interests of social elites rather than students from lower social class backgrounds. What becomes evident here is an elite strategy to downgrade social citizenship and impose a liberal model of citizenship upon an already divided and class-ridden society. This is less likely to serve the needs of 'fairness' than it is a social order where the privileged elite tend to go private schools, move on to the 'best' universities and then occupy the top positions in well-paid professions. This is of course the same class system that has become exaggerated by neoliberal reforms that promise massive wealth for the rich vis-à-vis job uncertainty, poor welfare services and the reduction of the public realm for the less well off. If the ConDems are keen to mystify this perception then it does not seem to have convinced the many concerned citizens who have taken part in wave of protests.

Finally, as an academic from a working-class background who found an intellectual home in the social sciences and the humanities, I am angered by the attempt to 'protect' priority areas (namely science and technology) and the related assumption that any other subject of study only becomes worthwhile if it can command large salaries in the future. My almost 20 years as a university lecturer has been driven not by money but by curiosity, intellectual passion and the idea that I might work with other staff and students who shared some of these values. Here I don't look back on the values of social democratic thinking as a kind of golden age but as a way of reminding ourselves that in recent human history we have been motivated by values other than those that can be derived from the market. As Martha Nussbaum demonstrates, the market model is far from neutral and in times of economic austerity aggressively acts against courses and subject areas that value critical thinking.[13] A world where the well-heeled study the humanities and social sciences while working-class students either struggle to get a job or study more vocational courses is one that would be recognisable to many social democratic writers of the recent past. If democratic societies require citizens who are capable of imaginatively thinking about how they wish to live, can think from the point of view of others and find value in dissenting voices then this is not well served by the new educational citizenship imposed by the present political elite.

NOTES

1. I. M. Young, *Inclusion and Democracy* (Oxford: Oxford University Press, 2000), p. 20.
2. C. Castoriadis, *Philosophy, Politics, Autonomy* (Oxford: Oxford University Press, 1991).
3. P. Toynbee, 'Some politicians lie, but this is unabashed mendacity', *The Guardian*, 8 January 2011, p. 31.
4. U. Beck, *Democracy Without Enemies* (Cambridge: Polity Press, 1998).
5. Ibid., p. 152.
6. A. Giddens, *The Third Way* (Cambridge: Polity Press, 1998).
7. Ibid., p. 72.
8. F. Mount, *Mind the Gap* (London: Short Books, 2004), p. 107.
9. J. Ranciere, *Hatred of Democracy* (London: Verso, 2006), p. 94.
10. M. Mann, 'Ruling class strategies and citizenship', *Sociology*, 1987, 21 (3), pp. 339–54.
11. S. Collini, 'Browne's gamble', *London Review of Books*, 32 (21), 4 November 2010, pp. 23–5.
12. D. Willetts, 'The system is fair and affordable', *Education Guardian*, 7 December 2010, p. 3.
13. M. Nussbaum, *Not For Profit* (Princeton: Princeton University Press, 2010).

Part III

Critical Pedagogy

8

The University as a Political Space

Alberto Toscano

Is it possible to democratise the university? This question, which has elicited divergent answers and numerous practical experiments over the past four or five decades, is once again on the agenda. But its parameters have changed. The 'mass university' of the 1960s and 1970s is not the corporate university of today, just as the apparently virtuous pattern of growth that underlay an earlier expansion of higher education contrasts with a zombie neo-liberalism that imposes austerity without being able to sell the idea of a real recovery to come.

Very schematically, among the principal drivers of the first global cycle of student revolts was the contradiction between the sociological 'democratisation' of universities – the selective integration into higher education of strata hitherto shut out of the sector, in keeping with the mutations of the labour market and national economic policies – and the 'feudal' character of power and privilege within these institutions. A glance at the demands of pre-68 student movements reveals a strong presence of a broadly social-democratic ideology of citizenship founded on labour and the collective good, mediated by appropriate forms of delegation and representation. A radical reformist vision of student participation in the forms of decision (university governance) and the intellectual content (curricula, definition of disciplines) was a fitting and immanent critique of the paternalist and technocratic discourse that accompanied the emergence of the mass university. Just as the wielders of the levers of power have invariably preferred theirs to be a managed democracy, so forms of self-management and autonomy have arisen by way of resistance. And when autonomy, maturity and critical reasoning are components of the ideology of an institution (today we could perhaps add creativity, innovation, and even radicalism), it is not surprising that some of its inhabitants 'over-identify' with them.

Now, if we extrapolate some commonalities from the cycle of university struggles in the years around 1968,[1] it is possible to note how quickly any vision of an internal, participatory reform of universities in a democratising direction was abandoned, in the face of entrenched authoritarianism (in many ways the key target of those movements), but also of the political demands posed by subjects, spaces and struggles beyond the university (anti-imperialist liberation movements, radical workers' struggles, feminism, radical black and minority movements, but also other authoritarian institutions, from the army to mental asylums). Brief as it may have been, however, the moment between the frustrated wish for participation and the abandonment of the university as a strategic, or even tactical, domain of struggle, remains rich with experiments and lessons – though not the kind to be simply transposed into the present. 'In and against' was the spirit of experiences such as the *Kritische Universität* in Berlin or the *Università Negativa* in Trento, experiences that were partly capable of combining the critique and transformation of educational content *and* form, taking the politically necessary time and space necessary to do so.

The question of power here served as the hinge between politics *in* the university, *against* the university and *beyond* the university. Just as it is well-nigh impossible to make antagonistic or emancipatory use of spaces and times without some practice of power, however organised, so the very act of posing the question 'who's in charge?' seems of necessity to push the politicisation of the university beyond its physical and institutional limits. The fate of the powerful watchword 'student power' testifies to this. In the preface to the eponymous 1969 collection promoted by the *New Left Review*, the tensions, impasses and potentials in this slogan are duly registered:

But, good or bad, all these impulses [for militancy or moderation] are manifestations of the revolution from below, along with hastily convened action committees; the discussion; the necessity, both in practical and psychological terms to control everything from lectures to telephones, to catering. All the more reason for the militants, in this atmosphere, to keep their heads: total control for a week, or a month, does not equal the capitulation of the enemy. But it does not mean, once the enemy has returned, that control was useless, or that the confrontation of the system on their own ground by students was a vain thing. ... [I]t is worth remembering that student power, often attacked as a limited and distorting phrase, still means what it says: the power of students to determine the structure and the content of their education. Of course the eventual aim is the cementing of a revolutionary bloc with working class forces; but the immediate power of the student lies in his university, his college, where he works as a student.[2]

This commendable strategic aim – to, in the Leninist parlance, create something like a 'dual power' in the university – was, some might say of necessity, short-lived, with some rushing to the 'eventual aim' and others retaking the path of piecemeal demands. In its student component, political action in universities appears thus as twice ephemeral: it rests on a relatively rapid turnover in its collective basis (as well as on the timing of teaching terms, exams, etc.), and it is drawn – in no small part by a critical vocation to map the social totality – beyond itself, to tackle greater authorities, to merge into broader struggles. The sociological imagination of the students at Nanterre, who were among the catalysts of the Parisian May, revealed as much: 'The unit of reference, the university, is not viable. The contradictions occur on the level of society as a whole, and the university is implicated in them.'[3]

But the fragile, transitory nature of student politics in a university can also be read as a strength: despite the segmented, and often instrumentalised, character of life in university institutions, they also allow for the fleeting if repeated formation of a peculiar form of collectivity. At once reflecting, and at times exacerbating, the divisions and contradictions in society at large, the university can also unify students in ways that corporativist or fragmented interests cannot. This has been acutely pointed out by the Spanish researcher Carlos Sevilla, who notes that 'students do not constitute a class, rather they find themselves situated in a temporal condition: they are apprentice intellectual workers who the moment they gain self-consciousness as a community are dispersed and find themselves neutralised. But in the brief interlude of their preparation they constitute a compact group which has demonstrated an enormous political impulse in country after country.'[4]

Precursor, catalyst, spark: student action has time and again, and long before '68, instigated wider, and at times less ephemeral, struggles – and although it is yet unclear to what extent the student rebellion against the ConDem attack on the universities will find relays in broader social movements, its political impulse was duly noted in the trade-unions: 'Britain's students have certainly put the trade union movement on the spot. Their mass protests against the tuition fees increase have refreshed the political parts a hundred debates, conferences and resolutions could not reach'.[5] Contrary to those who would wish to circumscribe it to representative channels over-determined by class power, economic resources and ideological inertia, democracy can also be the name for types of collective and direct action, such as occupations, which – while bypassing established 'democratic' procedures or being defined by authorities as illegal – generate from below their own forms of legitimacy.

But for all the analogies and continuities – if not in practices then at least in the challenges faced – to reflect on the possibility of democracy in the university today is also to confront a situation that harbours different potentials and throws up different limits to egalitarian and emancipatory collective action than the ones registered by previous movements. Most importantly perhaps, the powers we face are of a different nature: although the authority and ideology of a paternalistic state are not yet wholly defunct, they are now relayed by forms of control and measurement that take market competition as their model and use financial compulsion as their instrument – be it in shaping the university as a corporation or in disciplining students throughout their prospective 'working lives' via debt. With the by now familiar and perverse irony of neo-liberal governmentality – which banks on the idea of the individual as an entrepreneur of their inalienable (but thoroughly alienated) property, their 'human capital' – the further restructuring and de-funding of universities advertises itself as a new way of implementing 'the power of students to determine the structure and the content of their education'. In the words of the Browne review: 'Our proposals put students at the heart of the system. Popular HEIs [higher education institutions] will be able to expand to meet student demand. Students will be better informed about the range of options available to them. Their choices will shape the landscape of higher education.'[6]

Student Power 2.0 is a remarkable lesson in contemporary alienation: while collectively deprived of any meaningful power, and individually consigned to precariousness and anxiety, in their statistical existence as selective consumers students are now sovereign subjects! Thus, in the democracy of market competition, it makes perfect sense to posit that the student's 'choice' – for instance, not to face the burden of suffocating levels of debt – may 'democratically' imply the disappearance of numerous institutions, study places and jobs. The consumer-people will have chosen ...

If we take into consideration the truly anthropological impact of the commodification of subjectivity and its neo-liberal management, the pervasiveness of entrepreneurial models of the self and the social ban on collective solidarity, there is something pretty inspiring in the capacity of many members of this ephemeral class-that-is-not-a-class to rebel against their empowerment by Browne & co. Some credit, of course, should be given to the crisis and the consequent cracks in the shiny veneer of 'capitalist realism'.[7] That the ideology of the consumer-subject is a vast existential Ponzi scheme is beginning to dawn on many. But to see in this a re-edition of a lived experience of 'no future' would be insufficient. That is, unless we regard the mobilisation of students for demands that in many cases will make no difference to them personally (since the new fee and funding arrangements take effect after their graduation), as the formation of a solidarity between those who have no future – except one encompassed by debt and by the near-total absence of collective control over the spaces and times of everyday life.

If we wish to insist on the idea of democracy, this democratic content – collective egalitarian solidarity, and the imperative to take some measures of control over the conditions of social reproduction, against the illusions of personal choice – takes precedence over democratic form. By precedence, I do not mean that organisational and procedural questions fall by the wayside, but that, instead of being fetishistically treated as solutions in their own right, they come to be shaped by the attempt to have done with the individuated consumer, discovering forms of action determined by common needs and solidarities. In other words, 'the problem is not that of finding how to decide in common what we do, *but how to do that which can be the object of common decisions*, and *no longer to do* that which can only escape those who do it'.[8]

While the limits of a democratic reformism in the 1960s were set by the resistance of established authorities, the idea of a democratisation of decision-making processes within the university today encounters not just institutional and ideological but structural and financial obstacles. If the democratisation of the university is thought in a primarily procedural sense – say by increasing student and staff participation in decision-making processes now monopolised, in often opaque and pernicious ways, by 'senior management teams' – one risks facing the classic problem of workers' participation in management: gaining a 'say' in university budgets determined by punitive government policies may simply mean taking responsibility for administering scarcity. Moreover, in a sector forcibly restructured by Tory fantasies of anti-social Darwinism, common cause within an institution is as such perfectly compatible with attempts to undermine 'the competition' – i.e. colleagues and comrades in other institutions. This note of caution and scepticism about a certain idea of the democratic university is not meant to undermine efforts to contrast the new forms of power that pervade our institutions – forms all the more insidious in that, following New Public Management doctrines,[9] they have abandoned blunt authoritarianism for a capillary control of behaviour through ceaseless auditing, measurement and evaluation. On the contrary, a 'transitional programme' for a democratic university would certainly need to table collective measures against the kinds of managerial power that acts as a crucial transmission-belt for the implementation of government policies on education. In no particular order: repeal of charters that entrust university governance to unaccountable councils and trustees; capacity to control or veto budgetary decisions on the parts of students and staff; election and recall of senior management. In the current situation these 'non-reformist reforms'[10] would likely be laughed out of court as impossible – perhaps a testament to the fact that, contrary to certain misguided perceptions of reformism, meaningful procedural changes are in many ways more difficult than serious if fleeting experiences of democracy.

If we start from the latter, however, the notion of a democratic university is perhaps less daunting or mysterious. Though yet untranslated into powerful organisational forms, whether within or without the institution, the past few months (and, looking beyond the UK, the last decade or so) have seen a proliferation of collective actions that enact something like a democratisation from below.[11] Very significantly, and in marked contrast with earlier cycles of university struggles that responded to the authoritarian divide between lecturers and students, the combination of the drastic attack on universities and a shared experience of labour precariousness has permitted a rather unprecedented commonality of struggle (in no sense omnipresent, but nevertheless very real). Under its mild and innocent appearance, 'We support our lecturers' is potentially quite a subversive slogan (if reciprocated, and translated into a different practice of the university). These are solidarities that are still in a relatively embryonic form, and which have yet to be really extended in full to all workers in universities – where the hierarchy of labours, and the invisibility of many of them, is still as severe as anywhere else. That said, at a rank-and-file level, unions that had been disciplined into narrow if necessary corporativist activity, or symbolic campaigning, have begun, however slowly or patchily, to mutate into organs capable of supporting student action and beginning to pose substantial questions about the kind of university we want to work, learn and teach in.

These developments are both minor, in terms of the power exercised, and meaningful, since they elaborate, at the level of everyday life and work, practices and aspirations that are fundamentally at odds with the subordination of our activity to the imperatives of accumulation, competition and profit, and to the stultifying managerial practices that embody them. A democratic university could easily be declared an oxymoron: lecturers still exercise an extremely consequential power over students (their evaluations select them for the job market), mastery is arguably an ineliminable and necessarily undemocratic aspect of pedagogy, and, in an increasingly grave sense, access to universities, as well as the capacity to benefit from them when there, is not 'democratically' distributed. In spite of all this, though perhaps in part because of their continued inheritance of strangely pre-capitalist and non-instrumental principles, universities (with some considerable help from the government), have proven yet again to be incubators of a healthy indignation against the stripping of common and public resources to rescue an increasingly unequal, destructive and decrepit capitalism. It's not a vanguard, but it's a start.

NOTES

1. With inevitable distortion, I am drawing especially on the very rich and intense experience of the occupations at the University of Trento, whose documents, tracts and inquiries provide a great – and in some sense 'ideal-typical' – record of the trajectory from democratising reforms to the abandonment of the university as a strategic site for political action. See Movimento studentesco (ed.), *Documenti della rivolta universitaria* (Bari: Laterza, 1968/2008), pp. 1–113; Gerd-Rainer Horn, *The Spirit of '68: Rebellion in Western Europe and North America, 1956–1976* (Oxford: Oxford University Press, 2007), pp. 74–85.
2. Alexander Cockburn, 'Introduction', in Alexander Cockburn and Robin Blackburn (eds), *Student Power: Problems, Diagnosis, Action* (London: Penguin/New Left Review, 1969), pp. 13–14.

3. Daniel Cohn-Bendit, Jean-Pierre Duteuil, Bertrand Gérard, Bernard Granautier, 'Why sociologists?', in *Student Power*, pp. 377–8.

4. Carlos Sevilla, *La fábrica del conocimiento. La universidad-empresa en la produccíon flexible* (Madrid: El Viejo Topo, 2010), p. 152.

5. Len McCluskey, 'Unions, get set for battle', *The Guardian*, 19 December 2010, <http://www.guardian.co.uk/commentisfree/2010/dec/19/unions-students-strike-fight-cuts> [accessed on 4 March 2011].

6. *Securing a Sustainable Future for Higher Education: An Independent Review of Higher Education and Student Finance*, 12 October 2010, <http://www.bis.gov.uk/assets/biscore/corporate/docs/s/10-1208-securing-sustainable-higher-education-browne-report.pdf> [accessed on 4 March 2011].

7. Mark Fisher, *Capitalist Realism: Is There No Alternative* (Ropley: Zero Books, 2009). Fisher's book is an indispensable guide to the ideological and subjective complex that the recent movements in the UK have rebelled against. Its analysis of the lived experience of the measured is not the least of its contributions.

8. Gilles Dauvé and Karl Nesic, *Au-délà de la démocratie* (Paris: L'Harmattan, 2009), p. 24.

9. Gigi Roggero, *La produzione del sapere vivo. Crisi dell'università e trasformazione del lavoro tra le due sponde dell'Atlantico* (Verona: Ombre Corte, 2009).

10. André Gorz, *Strategy for Labor: A Radical Proposal* (Boston: Beacon Press, 1969).

11. A political experience of direct forms of democracy can thus be juxtaposed to the limited and limiting prospect of the university as a more democratic institution. In the wake of the rebellions of the late 1960s, Ernest Mandel made the following observation, in many respects still relevant: 'In the long run the university as an institution remains bound with golden chains to the power of the ruling class. Without a radical transformation of society itself the university cannot undergo any *lasting* radical transformation. But what is impossible for the university as an institution is possible for students as individuals and in groups. And what is possible for students as individuals and groups can, on the collective level, temporarily emerge as a possibility for the university as a whole.'

Ernest Mandel, 'The Changing Role of the Bourgeois University' (June 1970) (London: Spartacus League, 1971). Available at: <http://www.marxists.org/archive/mandel/1970/06/university.htm> [accessed on 6 March 2011]. On the idea of student co-management (as opposed to student *control*) of the university as a democratic mystification, see Mandel's *Les étudiants, les intellectuels et la lutte des classes* (Paris: La Brèche, 1979. Available at: <http://www.ernestmandel.org/fr/ecrits/txt/1979/etudiants/index.htm> [accessed on 6 March 2011].

9

The Academic as Truth-Teller

Michael Bailey

Writing in 1970 about 'The Business University', Edward Thompson envisaged a scenario in which 'dominant elements in the administration of a university had become so intimately enmeshed with the upper reaches of consumer capitalist society that they are actively twisting the purposes and procedures of the university away from those normally accepted in British universities, and thus threatening its integrity as a self-governing academic institution'.[1] But this was no work of fiction. The article was in fact a sarcastic broadside against Warwick University's close relations with industry and its authoritarian style of management. More specifically, Thompson was responding to the public disclosure that his then employer had been covertly 'scrutinising' members of its academic staff at the behest of one of its corporate benefactors – a local car manufacturer whose chairman also happened to be a co-opted member of the university's governing council. What is more, Thompson used the occasion to praise the student unrest that had enveloped Warwick since the late 1960s, in particular the actions of those students who occupied the university's registry and exposed the 'Warwick files' controversy in the first place.[2] And he was characteristically unequivocal about whose side academics ought to be on in the (albeit abstract) event that student dissent against the university's governing body should spread:

> If such a revolt were to occur, then the position of the university teacher would seem to be clear. He [*sic*] could not confine his role to that of making clucking protective noises on behalf of the rights or good intentions of his students. As an intellectual worker, in whatever field of study, he must

be unconditionally opposed to the mystification of truth ... He should
come to the side of the students by telling them what he knows of truth.[3]

Written some 40 years ago, Thompson's heartfelt polemic reminds
us that the encroaching corporatisation of higher education has
been long in the making. Also significant is his deep commitment to
the university's student body and his willingness to stand shoulder
to shoulder with students in their fight against an intransigent
management. But what stands out above all else, particularly in
the above passage, is Thompson's compelling sense of a moral
obligation to speak the truth and to expose corruption (no matter
how mild) when required. And it is this categorical imperative of
the academic as truth-teller that I especially want to focus on in
what follows. Not just because it is a topic worthy of discussion
in itself. But more importantly because it raises the question of
on what grounds and in what way should academics defend the
idea of adult higher education and academic independence in
the wake of the present crisis of capitalism and the concomitant
assault on education as a public good.

Of course, Thompson was no ordinary academic; indeed, he
spent just seven years working in higher education. First and
foremost, he was a committed activist and freelance writer who
cut his teeth teaching non-traditional learners in adult education.
And like many of his leftist contemporaries who answered the
vocational calling of the 'Great Tradition', Thompson was an
enthusiastic proponent of democratic scholarship and critical
pedagogy. He passionately believed that education ought to bear
some relationship to the lived experiences of ordinary people
as social beings and citizens, not as examinees or functionaries
of capitalism. Hence education should be about a free play of
the mind, a critical dialogue in which both teacher and student
jointly question received truths and established ways of thinking.
This is not to imply, however, that Thompson and the like
advocated that educator and student abandon intellectual rigor
and academic scholarship in the search for an entirely alternative
truth, or indeed with no regard for the truth whatsoever. The
excesses of so-called 'student-centred learning' are at best
relativist complacency, at worst university managerialism

gone mad. It is more a question of striking a judicious balance between education as the acquisition of objective knowledge and education as helping students realise their full potential for the greater good. Conceived in this way, education is of crucial importance for the fostering of a social consciousness, socio-cultural change and the gradual strengthening of the democratic process.

This last point is of vital importance in terms of the Manifesto outlined in the book's appendix and elsewhere. But what specifically of the academic as the teller of truth? And what sort of intellectual life should academics aspire to?

In attempting to answer these questions I want to begin with a series of lectures given by Michel Foucault at Berkeley in 1983.[4] The seminar was largely concerned with the Graeco-Roman conception of *parrhesia* or the relationship between belief and truth-telling. Foucault's main foci of interest, however, was not so much the problem of *what* constitutes the truth, but with the problematic of *who* is able to tell the truth and *why* one should tell the truth. Or, to be more precise, 'what are the moral, the ethical, and the spiritual conditions which entitle someone to present himself [sic] as, and to be considered as, a truth-teller?'[5] In other words, Foucault was less concerned with the analytics of truth than he was with a genealogy of the critical attitude to truth in early Western societies. And the overriding qualification discernible in much classical Greek literature, particularly philosophical treatises on *parrhesia*, is frankness of speech. In order to speak the truth one must speak as one finds, even if this involves a risk to oneself. Hence the condition that the *parrhesiastes* (the one who speaks truth) must be plain-speaking and avoid the use of rhetoric at all times. The objective is not that of persuasion or beguilement but the duty to speak honestly and courageously. Above all, *parrhesia* is an activity that requires one speak on behalf of others to those in positions of authority. But it is not enough to just preach or lecture others on what they should think or what they should do. Following the example of Socrates, there must also be a harmonic relation between what the *parrhesiastes* says (*logos*) and what she or he does (*bios*); the teller of truth must live by her or his word, which necessarily involves 'the cultivation of the self'.[6] Crucially, however, unlike neo-liberal notions of taking care of oneself, which prioritise laissez-faire individualism and self-responsibilisation, the Socratic idea of *epimeelia heautou* is altogether more ethical in so far as it raises not only the question of the relation between asceticism and truth but also the agonistic relationship between oneself and the well-being of the wider community.

Now, it goes without saying that one ought not look to some distant (and, one should add, far from democratic) Hellenistic ideal as a possible solution to contemporary socio-political issues. Besides, even the most committed teller of truth is doubtless guilty of the occasional falsehood or acting out of self-interest at some point in their life (such is the fallibility of human nature). Add to this Foucault's own ambivalent relationship with the role of the intellectual as the bearer of universal truths and we are faced with something of a philosophical conundrum.[7] Nevertheless, I want to suggest there is an enduring value in the commitment expressed in Foucault's rendering of *parrhesia*, especially the obligation to speak the truth for the common good. And I particularly want to stress the importance of truth-telling in terms of defending the (albeit relatively recent) idea of the university as a cornerstone for the realisation of an educated democracy, for two reasons.[8] First, the notion of *parrhesia* obliges public educators to live their lives in and through criticism (both self-criticism and criticism of others) and courage, not flattery or apathy. Furthermore, it is not enough for university lecturers and professors to seek truth through a monastic like withdrawal into the self; they must exercise an intellectual curiosity that is at once personal and social. In short, the academic as truth-teller has a moral responsibility to combine scholarship with critical thinking and civic duty.

It was precisely this spirit of radical pedagogy that inspired the late Edward Said to speak about the public role of writers and intellectuals when asked to deliver the prestigious Reith Lectures in 1993. Subsequently published as a collection of six essays titled *Representations of the Intellectual*, the thrust of Said's argument is that, not only is there such a thing as 'an intellectual vocation', more importantly, there is an ideal type of intellectual who confronts social injustices, is not afraid to exercise moral judgment and seeks to mobilise public opinion on behalf of socially disadvantaged groups. Hence his characterisation of the intellectual 'as exile and marginal, as amateur, and as the author of a language that tries to speak the truth to power'.[9] Of course, 'speaking truth to power' has become something of a cliché in academic discourse (though not as clichéd as 'knowledge is power') but the premise that intellectuals have a duty to *not* allow themselves to be co-opted by corporations and institutions of social authority is of crucial importance. For if one writes simply because writing pays a wage, or for professional kudos, there is a danger that intellectual content and critique will be sacrificed for presentation and conformity, political or otherwise.[10] Much better that the desire for (and dissemination of) knowledge is motivated by an independent spirit of enquiry, relentless erudition and a social conscience. And it is in this respect that Said's own intellectual legacy as academic-cum-truth-teller, not least his commitment to drawing public attention to the cause of the Palestinians and his criticism of US foreign policy, was nothing but exemplary.

Sadly, just as the principle of free higher education is under assault as never before, so too is the idea of the academic as a free-thinking intellectual, particularly in the UK. In the first place, rather than being allowed to pursue ideas for their own sake, increasingly British academics are pressured into meeting university and departmental demands for the five- or six-yearly Research Assessment Exercise (lately renamed the Research Excellence Framework). Introduced in 1985/6 as a means of evaluating the 'quality' of academic research across the various disciplines, the RAE requires university departments to submit four publications for each full-time member of staff selected for inclusion. Departments are then ranked according to their research outputs, research environment and indicators of esteem by a panel of subject specialists (there were 67 panels for the 2008 RAE). And it is these rankings that determine the allocation of quality weighted research funding each university receives from the Higher Education Funding Council for England

(HEFCE), a non-departmental public body currently overseen by the Secretary of State for the Department for Business, Innovation and Skills. But the pressure to perform well in the RAE has resulted in academics being subject to ever-increasing layers of micromanagement and performance indicators whose logic are more corporate than they are academic. In actual fact, the roots for this bureaucratisation of scholarship can be traced back to the elite US Ivy League business schools and management consultancy firms such as Bain & Company, the Boston Consulting Group and McKinsey.

The upshot of this academic drift is that the 'publish or perish' imperative is now endemic within academe. And not just any old publication will do. The sheer volume of submissions to the RAE (over 200,000 outputs were submitted as part of the 2008 RAE) makes it virtually impossible for panel members to read through each and every article, which invariably means that common assumptions are made about the 'quality' of articles published in top peer-reviewed journals vis-à-vis those published elsewhere. But what this supposition overlooks is all the very good quality research published by those academics who refuse to play the RAE 'game'. Indeed, it has been argued that only publishing in the 'top' journals forces academics to fashion their research around what those journals want, which can result in an unwillingness to push beyond the narrow confines of specialist fields of study and, ultimately, intellectual inertia.[11]

Moreover, with sails trimmed tight, increasingly academics are forced to cut corners if they are to meet the next publishing deadline, particularly newly qualified academics who are expected to combine research with heavy teaching loads and endless administrative duties (a problem whose sheer scale and mind-numbingly tedious and pointless nature appears to be exclusively British). 'What ever you do, don't over-prepare': 'You only need to be one step ahead': 'Just cover the basics, ignore the rest'. These are just some of the suggested coping strategies one encounters when starting a new lecturing post. So much for the idea that the university is a place where teaching is carried out in an atmosphere of research, and vice versa. And this says nothing of the way in which the instrumentalisation of research has undermined collegiality by atomising any sense of a collective academic community.[12] It is no wonder that many junior academics, though grateful to finally have got their feet under the desk, find the early years of their careers strangely alienating and dispiriting, not quite knowing where to begin, what to prioritise or who to turn to.[13]

Other 'McKinseyian' performance indicators include the unyielding pressures academics now face to secure external sources of funding (otherwise known as 'grant-capture'), which often involves the preparation of long and tedious application forms for ever decreasing amounts of money and worsening odds of success. To compound matters, most academic funding bodies have rolled out award schemes that encourage collaborative research with a non-academic partner, which necessarily means a further narrowing of research aims and objectives. That many present-day universities so prize 'cultural partnerships', 'corporate sponsorship' or 'third-stream funding' in an effort to offset the shortfall in government funding muddies the waters yet further insofar as one sees increasing numbers of academics posturing as 'consultants' in the belief that research which has an economic or technocratic function is the surest way to gain promotion. And should the forthcoming Research Excellence Framework go ahead with the proposed 25 per cent weighting for so-called 'impact' (the premise being that academics and university departments will need to demonstrate how their research has impacted on and benefited the wider economy and society) the situation will almost certainly become even worse. In terms of the humanities specifically, the effect would be, as recently noted by Stefan Collini, 'potentially disastrous', not least because the implication is that academics will 'be judged and rewarded as salesmen' and thus forced into 'hustling' and 'hawking' their intellectual wares.[14]

Of course, more 'enterprising' academics have embraced this market-oriented systemisation of research and have done very well for themselves. And some might say, 'more power to the elbow of those that succeed'. But universities and academics currying favour with big business and would-be private partners, as foretold by Thompson, is only the tip of the iceberg. At the time of going to press, the London School of Economics has been implicated in unscrupulous dealings to train members of Libya's future elite. In return, the university has received donations worth approximately £1.5 million from a 'charitable foundation' managed by Saif Gaddafi, son of the Libyan dictator, Colonel Muammar Gaddafi.[15] More curious still is the fact that Saif Gaddafi donated the money *after* the LSE awarded him a PhD. But rumour now has it that the PhD may have been plagiarised or even ghost written. Additionally, it is alleged that Anthony Giddens, LSE director 1996–2003, twice met with Muammar Gaddafi at the behest of Motor Group, a US lobbying firm that was paid more than £2 million by the Libyan government in 2006 to conduct a public relations campaign aimed at emphasising the emergence of a 'New Libya'.[16] In fact, Giddens is just one of a handful of influential academics and public intellectuals (others include Francis Fukuyama, Robert Putnam and Benjamin Barber) to have visited Tripoli in return for (undisclosed) honorarium payments.[17]

Not surprisingly, it has been suggested that the visits were about persuading Gaddafi to embrace political reform. On the other hand, speaking on behalf of his former LSE colleagues, Colin Talbot (now professor of public policy and management at the Manchester Business School) has revealed that Tony Blair's New Labour pressured educational institutions into opening up connections with Libya in the hope that this would foster closer economic relations.[18] Although there is probably an element of truth in Talbot's counter-argument,[19] there is strong evidence that certain member's of the LSE's governing body are deeply embroiled in political cronyism, British intelligence and (surprise, surprise) the oil industry.[20] Indeed, the Libya fiasco is just one of a series of similar cases where the LSE has accepted blood money from other Middle Eastern autocrats.[21] But what is truly shocking (and revealing) about the current controversy is the alarming number of eminent or promising LSE academics who have egg on their faces, not least David Held, professor of political science, who not only 'supervised' Saif Gaddafi's doctoral studies, but also invited him to give the 2010 Ralph Miliband memorial lecture on the grounds that he had 'come to know Saif as someone who looks to democracy, civil society and deep liberal values as the core of his inspiration'. Either Held knows something we do not (perhaps what Gaddafi Jnr really meant to promise his fellow citizens was 'rivers of love', not 'blood') or, as pointed out by Geoffrey Levy, he and his colleagues have been nothing but 'useful idiots'.[22]

Perhaps if Held and his colleagues had adopted more of a Socratic approach in their pedagogical relationship with Saif Gaddafi they would not be in the embarrassing situation they find themselves in presently. As it happens, their foolish actions tarnish not just the legacy of the LSE but also bring the very idea of the university and academic independence into disrepute. Such behaviour is inexcusable, and their colleagues should not hesitate to remind them of this. As for the LSE senior management and its board of advisors, one can reasonably surmise that their capacity for objective and honest decision making is deeply compromised, which is why it is incumbent upon the university's academic staff to tell what else they know of the truth, just as Edward Thompson did 40 years ago when confronted with a similar conflict of public and private interests. One certainly hopes that, should the pending independent inquiry (assuming it is not just whitewashing) show any senior manager, board member or academic to have acted improperly, the university will not hesitate to act accordingly, even if this means having to wash its dirty laundry in public. Whatever the outcome, the university's Academic Board should not hesitate to insist upon greater transparency and due process when matters concerning external relations and non-academic partnerships arise. Failure to do so would further undermine the university's credibility and, indeed, the much wider role that universities have to play in a democratic society.

Which brings us to the crux of the matter: as market-driven research and corporate partnerships are accorded even more importance in higher education due to ever decreasing amounts of public funding, it is increasingly likely that we will see yet more universities adopting a subordinate relationship with possibly corrupt and manipulative power elites. This is all the more reason for academics to adopt the position of truth-teller and to question anything and everything that facilitates the growing marketisation of higher education or undermines academic freedom. However, defending the university requires much more than academics representing truth through democratic criticism and moral indignation. Also needed is a much broader social movement comprising all UK university workers, students, other public sector employees and the trade unions. Only then might politicians start to rethink their present assault on higher education, indeed, on the welfare state at large.

In the meantime, it would seem that the onerous responsibility of speaking truth to power has fallen on the student movement. It is they who have taken the upper hand and who are asking difficult questions. And, who knows, *if* student occupations spread up and down the country, perhaps we will see the uncovering, just as Warwick's students did, of yet more evidence of ethical wrongdoing. If such a situation were to occur, however, universities will of course accuse students of irresponsible behaviour and do everything in their power to bring them to heel. In fact, there are already disturbing signs that the state itself may yet 'police' matters (in and through its many ideological apparatuses) should student dissent intensify. There is no question that those students singled out for 'public misconduct' in the months ahead risk all kinds of draconian sanctions, indeed, they run the risk of jeopardising their future careers. And all because they have the conviction to defend the idea of the university as a vital social and public institution. One only hopes that academics will express equal commitment and courage, not just in their writings, but in their actions too.

NOTES

1. E.P. Thompson, 'The business university', *New Society*, 19 February 1970; reprinted in *Writing by Candlelight* (London: Merlin, 1980), pp. 13–28.
2. For a fuller analysis of the 'Warwick files' controversy, see E.P. Thompson (ed.), *Warwick University Ltd: Industry, Management and the Universities* (Harmondsworth: Penguin Books, 1970).

3. Thompson, *Writing*, pp.15–16.
4. Michael Foucault, *Fearless Speech* (Los Angeles: Semiotext(e), 2001).
5. Ibid., p. 169.
6. Ibid., pp. 91–166. See also Michel Foucault, *The Care of the Self. The History of Sexuality: Volume Three* (London: Penguin Books, 1990).
7. Michael Foucault, 'Truth and power' in J.D. Faubion (ed.), *Essential Works of Foucault, 1954–1984. Volume 3: Power* (London: Penguin Books, 2002), pp. 111–33.
8. For a brief history of adult higher education, and its various institutional forms, see Stefan Collini, 'HiEdBiz', *London Review of Books*, 25 (21), 6 November 2003, pp. 3–9.
9. Edward W. Said, *Representations of the Intellectual* (New York: Vintage Books, 1994), p. xvi.
10. Ibid., p. 74
11. See Simon Head, 'The grim threat to British universities', *New York Review of Books*, 13 January 2011.
12. See Ronald Barnett, *Beyond All Reason: living ideology in the university* (Buckingham: Open University Press, in association with the Society for Research into Higher Education, 2003), pp. 108–10.
13. For a full analysis of the changing academic experience in the UK higher education sector (based on survey evidence), see Malcolm Tight, *The Development of Higher Education in the United Kingdom since 1945* (Berkshire: Open University Press, 2009), pp. 271–97.
14. Stefan Collini, 'Impact on humanities', *Times Literary Supplement*, 13 November 2009, pp. 18–19.
15. Jeevan Vasagar and Rajeev Syal, 'LSE head quits over Gaddafi scandal', *The Guardian*, 3 March 2011: http://www.guardian.co.uk/education/2011/mar/03/lse-director-resigns-gaddafi-scandal [accessed 5 March 2011].
16. Rajeev Syal & Jeevan Vasagar, 'Anthony Giddens' trip to see Gaddafi vetted by Libyan intelligence chief', *The Guardian*, 4 March 2011: http://www.guardian.co.uk/education/2011/mar/04/lse-libya-anthony-giddens-gaddafi [accessed 5 March 2011].
17. Ed Pilkington, 'The Monitor Group: Gaddafi's PR firm used academics', *The Guardian*, 4 March 2011: http://www.guardian.

co.uk/world/2011/mar/04/the-monitor-group-gadaffi-pr [accessed 5 March 2011].

18. Jeevan Vasagar & Rajeev Syal, 'British government encouraged LSE to forge Libya links, says academic', *The Guardian*, 4 March 2011: http://www.guardian.co.uk/education/2011/mar/04/lse-british-government-libya-links [accessed 5 March 2011].

19. See Susil Gupta 'Qaddafi and the London School of Economics: Libya and the Hand That Feeds', *counterpunch*, 2 March 2011: http://www.counterpunch.org/gupta03022011.html [accessed 5 March 2011].

20. Geoffrey Levy, 'London School of Useful Idiots: How a cadre of Blair cronies, ex-MI6 chiefs and top dons at a top university supported Gaddafi for his millions', *Daily Mail*, 2 March 2011: http://www.dailymail.co.uk/news/article-1362029/Gaddafi-supported-Blairs-cronies-ex-MI6-chiefs-LSE-millions.html#ixzz1FTzZp8K6 [accessed 5 March 2011].

21. Emmanuel Akpan-Inwang, 'The LSE's Libya connection is only the tip of the iceberg', *The Guardian*, 4 March 2011: http://www.guardian.co.uk/commentisfree/2011/mar/04/lse-howard-davies-libya-uae [accessed 5 March 2011].

22. Levy, *Daily Mail*, 2 March 2011.

10
Impoverished Pedagogy, Privatised Practice

Natalie Fenton

The current attacks on higher education in the UK are far from new. They represent a long gradual slide to reduce the role of state funding in tertiary education that plummeted in the 1990s when the amount of funding per student fell by 40 per cent, largely due to the expansion in student numbers;[1] the introduction of student fees in the decade that followed helped a seriously underfunded system, but government funding has continued the downward trajectory, indeed, we are faced with an alarmingly steep downhill (that feels more like a precipice) ending with an almighty crash (that will be fatal for some) with the withdrawal of 80 per cent of government funding for teaching (roughly £3.9 billion) from 2012. As the disciplines of science, technology, engineering and medicine are to be protected (although still facing some cuts), this will mean a total withdrawal of public subsidy for the arts, humanities and social sciences – with a massive hike in student fees of up to £9,000 expected to fill the shortfall. Only the government is not expecting most universities to charge enough to replace the funding withdrawn, it is in fact advising against it. Rather, it is expecting to see major 'efficiencies' in a system that will have to change beyond all recognition in a newly privatised funding regime.

These changes will have a massive impact on universities in general and on teaching in particular as we see a decisive move away from the notion of the university as a public good of necessary general benefit to society, funded largely through public funds (except for the elite few); to university education as another commodity in a lightly regulated market in which consumer demand drives the unit of production (previously known as the provision of higher education through universities) for the benefit of private individuals. This is not so much a 'cut' in funding as it is a complete re-classification of what a university should be, which has enormous ramifications for the jobs that we do and the education we are engaged in.

The irony of course is that the government are trying to sell their proposals on the basis that the market will deliver better quality university education. The Browne report on which the proposals are based states that 'students are best placed to make the judgment about what they want to get from participating in higher education'. His oft repeated phrase is 'student choice will drive up quality,' and the measure of quality is 'student satisfaction'. He bemoans the fact that in the current system 'students do not have the opportunity to choose between institutions in terms of price and value for money.' Under his proposals all this will change, with value being judged primarily by students in terms of 'the employment returns from their courses'. In other words, courses that lead to higher earnings will be able to charge higher fees. This sounds less like student choice and more like neoliberal ideology. The same principles underpin the repayment scheme: 'Graduates will be required to make a greater contribution to the costs of higher education varying widely according to how much benefit they have received from studying', where the amount of benefit is solely predicated on the size of their salary. Consequently, we are told, 'increasing competition for students will mean that institutions will have stronger incentives to focus on improving teaching quality. If they are not able to attract enough students, their funding will decrease,' and ultimately they will close – and closures are expected. To prevent such drastic action universities are 'encouraged' to make ever more 'efficiencies'. The assumption is that the majority of universities will be operating on less money than they are now (some on far less).[2]

What might these efficiencies look like in these freshly privatised institutions? Some institutions are already rushing headfirst into two-year degrees – this means either squashing 90 weeks of teaching into two years with two weeks off at

Christmas and Easter and three weeks in the summer, or offering a sub-degree education but charging more. There are clear educational (and moral) concerns with this approach. Many students' blossom in the third year of their degree as all the reading and all the courses finally come together and start to mean something bigger than the individual parts. Having acted as an external examiner in several institutions I see over and over again how students flourish in their final year as their grades improve and they finally begin to realise their potential. Mature writing skills, learning how to think, debate, critique, developing historical consciousness and diverse understandings have no quick-fix option.

The issues for teaching staff are equally detrimental. Cramming teaching into every available hour to maximise space utilisation and student turnover is a recipe for demoralisation, demotivation and stagnation. Cramming short courses for industry into the summer removes any chance of research, writing or even reading. Research-led teaching will increasingly become a luxury for all but the few elite institutions charging the highest fees. No one will be able to keep up to date with the latest research, develop new research proposals or even read the books that pile high on the desk throughout term time, let alone do any empirical research or writing themselves. Teaching will inevitably suffer. In these newly 'efficient times' when does a lecturer mark those 150 x 5,000 word scripts, revise old courses or develop new ones? Presumably, the marking speeds up as feedback is spread thin and those old courses, well they simply stay as those old courses. The irony is, of course, that students may not spot the weaknesses themselves as they are not best placed to judge whether or not a lecturer has a complete grasp of their field. You can score highly on student feedback based almost entirely on style and entertainment value over substance and erudition. Moreover, if you give out bad grades you run the risk of direct translation into negative student feedback. The nonsense of performance-related pay index-linked to grades suddenly looks like a genuine possibility in the university supermarket. While the National Student Survey gains in importance as the consumer guide to acquiring a degree it is all too easy to see how purchasing power can override pedagogic sense.

In the interest of efficiency it is also likely that universities will come to rely increasingly on fixed term and hourly paid staff for delivering courses – the Cinderellas of the system, propping up under-staffed departments. They are, after all, relatively cheap and easily exploitable in a market where established posts become ever more of a rarity. In many institutions, hourly-paid staff have become critical to the delivery of core modules, are valued as colleagues and often teach for many years, but receive no job security and precious little reward. This is no longer essential early career experience for those fresh from doing their PhD, rather it has become institutionalised exploitation. Hourly paid staff suffer some of the worst employment conditions in the sector – often they have no office, no workplace computer, no access to staff meetings or training and development courses and are not paid properly for the work that they do (frequently preparation time is either not paid for or severely underestimated and paid-for tutorial time grossly inadequate). From the student perspective, hourly-paid staff may be more difficult to get hold of and are less likely to have the same detailed knowledge of institutional regulations and the intricacies of the curriculum. They are also, of course, more likely to leave.

Ultimately, when the funding squeeze is so severe the axe eventually (or sometimes all too soon) falls on established staff. Less staff doing more work for less pay is usually where 'efficiency drives' end up. When pathetic voluntary severance packages fail to reap dividends, institutions move to other measures such as a freeze on posts. When the freeze on posts fails to impact on the bottom line then the wage bill has to fall through compulsory redundancies. Those lucky enough to still have a job have to mop up the workloads left behind, often massively increasing teaching hours on those new postgraduate courses brought on stream to generate more funding. Frequently, job freezes and voluntary and compulsory redundancies are targeted at academic-related staff in the misconception that these roles are more dispensable, leaving a paucity of administrative support to carry out basic procedures heaping yet further administrative workloads on all those left behind – academic and academic-related staff alike. For academic staff, more administration creates yet further distance from students and less time for preparation, marking and pastoral care.

Another common 'efficiency' already being employed as institutions struggle to survive is the cutting of all programmes that currently have less than a certain number of students registered on them or can't guarantee that they can attract a certain number to them or indeed require rather more intensive teaching practice. Places differ slightly on where the line in the sand is drawn but the principle remains the same – maximise student numbers while minimising human resource (previously known as lecturers). When applying market logic this may make sense but in an educational context it means waving goodbye to those specialist degrees that recruit steadily but not in mega-numbers or those courses that are more labour intensive. It will lead to a greater concentration in subject areas that are more profitable and least expensive as provision responds to market demand. It will also inhibit risk-taking in imaginative courses lacking a sound 'business case'. While students are saddled with huge fees to give them 'choice' and thousands are priced out of university altogether, subjects without self-evident 'market value' face extinction. The range of degrees on offer will narrow, the types of subjects available within degree programmes will diminish and real choice will be increasingly limited.

Since the introduction of fees in 2004 university educators have become used to the consumer rhetoric of choice and demand. But the increased competition about to be unleashed upon us will take this to another level. As full-fee-paying customers, students will increasingly complain that the product they are buying doesn't meet the requirements of the Trades Description Act or is simply faulty. Students are being encouraged to see a tripling of fees in terms of the quality of the product where quality is judged on measurable outcomes. Increasingly the faults students point to will be directed at the grades they are given. This is entirely understandable in a situation where the need to get a highly paid job to pay off the mountain of debt they are accumulating means that anything less than a 2:1 does not represent value for money. Litigation by students will surge and the pressure on lecturers to play it safe and avoid the risks of being innovative or adventurous will be high.

Student debt will be a driver in another direction. All but the most affluent will be induced to turn away from courses in literature, history, philosophy, art, design, media and social sciences and towards professional qualifications in 'high-utility' subjects such as law and business administration in the hope of a certain return for the liability they are about to be burdened with. Some institutions have already cut teaching in the humanities (such as the closure of History and planned closure of Philosophy at Middlesex University, along with the severe cutbacks to English), a trend that will continue until subjects such as history and philosophy become the preserve, once again, of the privileged.

Universities have been operating on an impoverished funding basis for quite some time, but contained within the parameters of being public institutions. In practice this has meant that the teaching grant has enabled institutions to maintain less popular subjects while also providing a certain level of financial stability. Furthermore, fees have not been determined by the actual cost of the student's education, since these vary between courses and between universities. This has enabled us to build our institutions based on educational priorities that are accepted as being for the common good and in the public interest. Privatising university teaching destroys those shared purposes and devalues knowledge that is not utility oriented and contoured towards corporate ends.

Privatisation of public universities also means narrowed student access and expanded inequalities (despite attempts to argue otherwise). This too will have a direct impact on teaching. There is the obvious issue of the least well off simply finding it inconceivable that they could shoulder such huge levels of debt while the more privileged have a cushion of family wealth to ease the discomfort. In the past two to three decades there have been huge advances in turning higher education from an elite system to a mass system for enormous democratic gain. These gains are now under serious threat. As the first person in my family ever to go on to higher education I, for one, know that option would never have been available to me on the proposed fee levels, yet neither would I have been eligible for the grants proposed for the poorest. And while it is true that there are proposals for a National Scholarships Programme to provide grants for those with family incomes below £25,000 and partial grants for those below £42,000, the scrapping of the Educational Maintenance Allowance that enables the poorest to stay in post-16 education makes a mockery of any attempts at fair access as Martin Harris, Director of Office for Fair Access, readily acknowledges.

But even if you do get to the point where you can apply to university, the newly inflated market will mean that elite institutions will recruit students from privileged backgrounds on the highest fees and be able to provide the most well-resourced learning environment; while those institutions that traditionally attract less privileged students will have to set their fees much lower, requiring more students and/or less staff to fill the funding shortfall. It is likely that staff–student ratios will differ wildly between these institutions and the quality of education on offer will diverge far more than it already does. It is the final drive towards a decade-long aim to bring back research intensive institutions at one end and teaching factories at the other. No prizes for guessing which end of the social spectrum suffers the most.

Of course those institutions that charge over £6,000 will have to show that they are making every effort to meet widening participation targets, but many believe their current efforts will already suffice in this regard. Things will not get better; higher education will not be fairer. It will be more unequal in every way. And this has a direct impact on the teaching context. Understanding, tolerance and informed judgement usually increase when students are faced with peers who are from mixed backgrounds rather than those who most resemble themselves. Such diversity will become increasingly difficult to maintain. Scholarship programmes or fee waivers for widening participation will be the new sticking plasters on a desperately broken system.

CONCLUSION

The brutal enforcement of market principles into every aspect of higher education is a direct attack on equality and the value of public education for all. It is a turn away from equality of opportunity and a rush towards students as units of revenue and departments as profit centres. Our universities will increasingly be driven by purchase power rather than by who belongs in them or whom a public institution is meant to serve. It will threaten an education system that is rich, deep, broad and critical. Though already corporatised on many levels, universities are still public institutions and their arts, humanities and social science departments are some of the last places that can challenge the principle that our lives can and should be ordered primarily by economic utility. It is in these departments that such practice is subject to critique; where we can trace its history, theorise its power, calculate its destructiveness and then seek to express our concerns in art, film and poetry. Perhaps we should not be surprised that these areas are most under attack. But if we value higher education and learning for the public good and in the public interest, if we value higher education as a route to social justice, if we value higher education as a means to increase understanding then we must protect its public heritage and defend tenaciously the right to think.

NOTES

1. S. Collini, 'Browne's Gamble', *London Review of Books*, 32 (21), 4 November 2010.
2. The Browne Report, 'Securing a Sustainable Future for Higher Education'. Available at: http://hereview.independent.gov.uk/hereview/

Part IV

Student Politics

11

Student Revolts Then and Now

John Rees

Hundreds of thousands of students were involved in marches and college occupations in the last months of 2010. They are the latest student generation to be involved in radical politics. Most student movements since the Second World War have been radical and progressive. But it wasn't always this way. Before the war the university system, both in Britain and throughout the world, was for the wealthy elite. Only small numbers got to university at all, and they were overwhelmingly the sons and daughters of the rich. Whatever their educational vocation, what they were also being taught was to be the next generation of rulers. So when there was any social conflict or division, the majority of students would side with the political elite. This was the way it was in the British General Strike of 1926. The government organised volunteers to scab on the strike by keeping the transport system running. Students were prominent, if not very effective, among the volunteers.

In Germany in the following decade students were as likely to support the Nazis as they were to oppose them. Indeed, students participated in the notorious book burnings organised by the Nazi SA. One American observer recorded:

Here the heap grew higher and higher, and every few minutes another howling mob arrived, adding more books to the impressive pyre. Then, as night fell, students from the university, mobilized by the little doctor [Goebbels], performed veritable Indian dances and incantations as the flames began to soar skyward.[1]

There was little opposition to the Nazis from the Deutsche Studentenschaft, the student organization to which all German

University students had to belong. Some of its members even tried to 'out-Nazi' Hitler's rival student organisation.

Nevertheless, there was opposition to the Nazis from a minority of German students. Hans and Sophie Scholl and their White Rose organisation scattered anti-Nazi leaflets around Munich University, including the main atrium of the university itself. They were caught by the Gestapo and beheaded in 1943. In the same year one of their leaflets that had been smuggled out of Germany was reproduced and dropped by Allied planes over Germany.

It was the post-war expansion of university education in the 1950s and 1960s that really transformed student politics. University was certainly not open to most working-class children even after this expansion had taken place. But the minority of working class students was larger and the number of middle-class students, as opposed to students coming from the real elite, was significantly enlarged.

The rapidly growing capitalist economies needed a larger educated stratum of mangers, officials, technocrats, teachers and professionals. University education was expanded to meet this need. In 1940 there were just 69,000 students in Britain. That figure had doubled by 1954. Ten years later it had doubled again to 294,000. In the next eight years this figure more than doubled again to reach around 600,000 by 1972. Now there are over two million students studying in higher education, making up more than 45 per cent of their age group.[2]

As they expanded the universities began to change in character. Education was no longer the leisurely amateur pursuit of a small highly privileged minority. Now education became more standardised. It was a mass product, not a craftsman's product. Universities became more like factories designed to turn out this product.

1956 HUNGARY: STUDENTS AGAINST STALINISM

One of the first and most significant student revolts of the post-war period came not in the West but in the Stalinist east.

Students were the detonator of the Hungarian revolution of 1956. Opposition to the government in Hungary first appeared as a solidarity movement with the political reforms that were taking place in Poland. There the thaw that began in the Eastern bloc after Stalin's death in 1953 had produced a reform minded government under Gomulka.

On 22 October student meetings adopted a resolution calling for the withdrawal of Soviet troops and called for a mass demonstration the following day 'in solidarity with our Polish brothers'.[3] At first the government gave permission for the demonstration. It even allowed the details to be broadcast on the radio. In Budapest the walls, trees and hoardings were covered with the students' placards. Crowds formed around them discussing the coming demonstration. Then the government changed its mind and withdrew permission for the demonstration. This only made it look weak and increased the students' determination.

As the demonstrations began from different parts of the city the government knew that it could not stop them. There were 100,000 on the streets. And more still were arriving. Later, after listening to speeches, some protestors toppled the statue of Stalin in the city park. Then they headed for the radio station, where they were met by 500 armed political police, the AVH. The police used tear gas which only blew back in their face. The crowd surged forward again and a police machine gun was fired. Some demonstrators fell to the ground, but others fought back with stones and petrol bombs and, because off-duty police and Home Guard officers were in the crowd, they had guns.

The fighting spread throughout Budapest. Workers ran to their factories to gather their friends and to get weapons from the factory sports clubs. A revolution had started. Workers' councils and revolutionary committees would soon spring up across Hungary. The revolution would only be halted by Russian tanks ... and the deaths of 20,000 Hungarians.

1960s STUDENTS AND THE US CIVIL RIGHTS MOVEMENT

The next peak of student radicalism took place in the 1960s, in the heart of Western capitalism, the USA. The Civil Rights movement was a conflict between the black population of the USA and the endemic racism of US society, especially in the southern states. Here racist laws and racist attitudes born on the slave plantations before the American Civil War still lived on.

In 1960 the US Supreme Court ruled in the case of Boynton versus Virginia that it was against the law for there to be racial segregation in the restaurants and waiting rooms in terminals serving buses that crossed state lines. It was already supposed to be illegal on the inter-state buses themselves. The Freedom Rides that started in 1961 were designed to test the law.

Increasing numbers of Freedom Riders took the bus into the south, many of them students who, when they got there, organised Freedom Schools to compensate for the racist education system and voter registration campaigns to ensure that blacks weren't terrorised out of exercising their democratic rights. They became part of the Civil Rights movement, whose figurehead was Martin Luther King.

As the Civil Rights movement gained in strength the new mood began to affect whole campuses, not just the minority from the colleges who went south. And students began to raise their own issues, as well as fight for the civil rights of others. In 1964, the year of the Freedom Summer in the south, the Berkeley campus in San Francisco exploded. Student Mario Savio was addressing 6,000 students having just heard that he might be expelled for his part in a demonstration two months before. Part of the crowd occupied the college, which was cleared by police who arrested 800 students. As they sat in the cells, between 60 and 80 per cent of the student body of 30,000 staged a strike. It was a sign of things to come, and not just in America.

THE 1968 STUDENT REVOLUTION

1968 has become known as the year of student revolution. Certainly students were in the forefront of the battles of that year, but it would be quite wrong to imagine that they were the only force that made 1968 a watershed year given, for example, the war in Vietnam and the democracy movement in

Czechoslovakia. But student protests went off like fire-crackers around the globe: Poland, Mexico, the USA, Germany, Italy, France, Brazil, Spain, Britain. In Berlin 10,000 students held a sit-in to protest over the Vietnam war. In March, the University of Rome was closed for twelve days by an anti-war protest. The same month the Grosvenor Square demonstration in London ended with 86 injured and 200 arrested. And again in March military police in Brazil killed a high school student who was protesting in favour of cheaper meals for poor students. That sparked a movement against the military government of Brazil. In Madrid the University was closed by protest for 38 days after a Catholic mass was said for Adolf Hitler.

The French movement was part of the global upsurge, concerned with Vietnam and civil rights, but it also had local origins. French universities were growing and overcrowded and their internal regime was, like the French state, authoritarian. The French student movement had been building up for some time, although until May 1968 relatively small numbers were involved. It was the minister of education's decision to close the whole of the University of Paris and send in the riot police to clear protesters from the Sorbonne that escalated the protest. On 6 May, students were battling with riot police in the Latin Quarter of Paris. The rioting dominated the news: student protest had become a national crisis. On 8 May the leaders of the Paris trade unions joined the demonstrations. Then came the night of 10 May, the Night of the Barricades. As police tried to bottle up protesters in the streets around Boulevard Saint Michel the protesters responded by turning the area into a police-free zone, erecting barricades of overturned cars, barbed wire and building materials. The government ordered the police in and hours of street battles lasted through the night. Now a crucial change in the balance of forces took place. The leaders of the major trade unions had been meeting that night. They listened, horrified, to the reports as they came in and decided to call a general strike for the following Monday, 13 May.

This general strike and mass demonstration on that day marked the transition from a student uprising to a working-class revolt. The next day in Nantes, at the Sud Aviation factory, where weekly symbolic strikes of 15 minutes to protest the cut in hours and wages had been going on for months, young workers under Trotskyist and anarchist influence refused to return to work after the 15-minute stoppage. They marched through the factory, feeling confident as a result of the biggest working-class demonstration since the liberation of France.

At the Renault plant in Cléon, the young workers did the exact same thing. The day after that, the strike spread to all of the Renault plants – six in total. That night, the main Renault plant at Billancourt, the largest factory in France, employing 35,000 people, the most militant and historically important factory in France, was occupied. A full-scale general strike was under way. Eventually only the dissolution of the government and fresh elections could end the crisis.

A number of salient points stand out in this account: first, it was the French state's decision to send the police on to the occupied campuses that first accelerated the student struggle. Second, it was the intensity of the student struggle – its stamina, militancy, political character and determination to confront the police – that first mobilised workers, not some artificial horizontal link between the left in the unions and the student movement. Third, it was mass *official* action by the unions in calling the demonstrations and the general strike that preceded the spreading of *unofficial* action.

THE STUDENT MOVEMENT OF 2010

The student movement of 2010 was the largest for a generation. It transformed the political atmosphere around the Tory–Liberal Democrat Coalition government's cuts programme and popularised the 'rejectionist' argument that the deficit could be paid for by taxing the rich, the corporations, and the banks or by cutting Trident and the war budget for Afghanistan. It undermined the legitimacy of the government by exposing a larger democratic deficit: the election of 2010 had revealed an electorate that voted centre left, but the government they got was monetarist and right wing.

So what led to the rise of this transformative movement? In the broadest sense the student movement was prefigured by the anti-globalisation movement that was born at the Seattle World Trade Organization conference in 1999. For a decade anti-corporate, anti-capitalist values and popular demonstrations that express these sentiments have been part of political life. They have left their mark on the attitudes and shaped the political participation of a generation of young people. The anti-global-isation movement, especially in Britain, fed into the anti-war movement as it arose after the attack on the World Trade Centre in 2001. Mass anti-war demonstrations, large-scale political rallies, pickets and protests have provided a vehicle for political action for young people over this period.

In particular the first modern mass action by school students took place as part of the Stop the War Coalition's campaign against the Iraq war. In the days around the outbreak of war in 2003 school students struck and walked out to join protests and marches against the war. A minority of them directly organised School Students Against the War. This organisation had been reformed by a new generation of school students six months before the fees protests and the individuals in this organisation were part of the fees protest as well.

Many of the first generation of school students had, of course, gone on to be university students in their own right in the period after 2003. At university they continued to participate in anti war activity and were galvanised by events such as the Israeli attack on Gaza at the start of 2010 (see Chapter 12). So the generation of students that confronted the new ConDem government in 2010 contained some considerable numbers who had direct experience of protest and action of a highly politicised kind. Moreover, there existed a decade-long experience of such action, perhaps taken by their old brothers, sisters, relatives and friends, which shaped the environment in which they had come of age.

In response to the ConDem government's plans to increase tuition fees and scrap the Education Maintenance Allowance (EMA), a series of demonstrations, protests and occupations were launched in the last two months of 2010. Many myths have flowered around the student movement that both helped to build and emerged from these events. It is said that it was a spontaneous revolt, without official leadership. It is said that it was all organised on the new social media. It is said by some that it was mainly school students who demonstrated, while others have claimed it to be a movement of university students. The truth about the student demonstrations is that they happened on the scale they did because of a mixture of official and unofficial organisation. The first demonstration on 10 November 2010 could never have been the size that it was without the official organisation and legitimacy imparted to it by the NUS and the UCU. At the Millbank Tower a militant minority, albeit a very large minority of some many thousands, gave the action on the day a character that the official unions did not imagine existed and did not like when it was expressed. Nevertheless, without the official call the demonstration would not have had the size it had and the minority of militants would not have gathered the support they needed to take effective action.

The two subsequent, mainly school student demonstrations, built on the impetus created by the first demonstration and they were popularised using Facebook and Twitter. But they also relied on unofficial networks created from the first demo and on the intervention of militants organized at ULU, in the National Campaign Against Fees and Cuts and, to a lesser degree, the Education Activists Network. The final and second biggest demonstration, benefited from the limited call given by the NUS and UCU but it was overwhelmingly the work of ULU and the unofficial campaigns whose organised base was significantly widened by the widespread occupations of the colleges taking place at the same time. In this demonstration university students once again outnumbered school students.

The action of the school students was in many ways the most exciting and visible part of the campaign. But the organisation by university students, with the capacities of their local unions and occupations to draw on, was essential in giving the movement politics, strategy and stamina. The shock troops came from the schools, but the organisational capacity, the logistics, the ability to deal with the police, courts and the media, came from university students.

The wave of university occupations significantly added to the student's organisational capacity. As we shall see in the next chapter, they were bases from which wider involvement could be galvanised. They were centres of political debate and places where the next demonstration could be prepared and, crucially, they brought the debate about fees to the door of the college administrations who were to implement it on behalf of the government.

WORKERS AND STUDENTS

The student struggle of 2010 was immediately effective in dividing the Liberal Democrats. LibDem ministers voted for the fees rise, some LibDem MPs abstained, others voted against the proposal. The *Daily Telegraph* chose this moment to attack the LibDems over the 'Cablegate' interview in which two undercover reporters encouraged Vince Cable into some bragging about his opposition to Rupert Murdoch's expansion of his media empire. LibDems slid in the polls from 22 per cent support at the election to 12 per cent, even as low as 8 per cent in some polls.[4] The government as a whole won the vote but it lost the argument and its stock with the electorate slumped. In polls after the student demonstrations Labour was ahead of the Tories for the first time since the election.

Union leaders from Bob Crow and Mark Serwotka to Len McCluskey, the newly elected leader of the country's biggest union, Unite, praised the students and urged trade unionists to follow their example. But would they? This was the question being asked across British society. In many minds the precedent of 1968 was being recalled. Then, as we have seen, a student struggle had detonated a general strike in France and, on a slower timescale, it was the precursor of workers' struggles in Britain. But, as we have also seen, it was the intensity of the student struggles that first led to official action by the unions and this, in turn, led to unofficial action on a wide scale. The myth of students simply 'calling workers out' or of 'unofficial action' simply spreading as a result of student–worker contact underestimates the complexity of events and so disarms those who today wish to generate a higher level of working class resistance based on the student struggles.

The student movement that emerged in 2010 is the biggest in Britain for a generation, but it is not yet bigger than it was in France in 1968. The first task in the coming period is to sustain and intensify this struggle. This is not because very many today share the illusion of some on the far left in 1968 that the students can build 'red bases' in the colleges that will be sufficient to challenge the government on their own but because the key to the involvement of workers lies, in the first instance, in the intensity of the student struggle. Artificial attempts to 'link with the workers' will not necessarily help because trade union struggles move at a different pace than those among students. The students can, however, cause a social crisis into which workers, organised and unorganised, are drawn. But for this to happen the student struggle itself, the occupations and demonstrations, need to be sustained and spread. The trade unionists in the education unions will find it easier to become involved in the struggle if this is the case, and this can be a bridge to other workers becoming involved. Occupations are key to this because they make the campuses ungovernable for the university authorities and present the staff with the question of taking sides in a way that demonstrations alone do not.

NOTES

1. Quoted in Jeremy Noakes and Geoffrey Pridham (eds), *Nazism, 1919–1945*, Vol. 2: *State, Economy and Society 1933–1939* (Exeter: University of Exeter Press, 2000), p. 207.
2. Universities UK, *Higher education in facts and figures* (London: UUK, 2010), pp. 5–6.
3. *Report of the Special Committee on the Problem of Hungary,* UN General Assembly, Official Records: Eleventh Session, Supplement No. 18 (A/3592) p. 69.
4. YouGov, Gov't trackers—update 8 December 2010. Available at: http://today.yougov.co.uk/politics/govt-trackers-update-8th-dec [accessed 18 February 2011].

12

The Politics of Occupation

Feyzi Ismail

The student movement that spread across Britain towards the end of 2010 will be remembered for igniting the fightback against the ConDem government. The university occupations over fees and cuts were a central component of this movement and, together with the demonstrations, gave it vitality, momentum and strategic direction. While it was the initial demonstration of 10 November that gave confidence to students to organise the occupations, growing support for the occupations within universities gave the movement its defiance and determination, forcing open the possibility of resistance not just to fee increases but to the whole government austerity plan. The occupations also played a major role in generating and sustaining a rank and file student organisation, which ensured that after the National Union of Students (NUS) pulled away from organising demonstrations, mass action could be coordinated by the grassroots. Ultimately, despite Parliament voting on 9 December 2010 to increase tuition fees, the movement was successful in exposing the ConDem government's ideological support for bank bailouts on the one hand and its refusal to fund a welfare state worthy of public support on the other.

University occupations across Britain had taken place in the recent past. There were some 27 occupations in protest at the Israeli assault on Gaza in early 2009, many of which won scholarships for Palestinian students and public statements by managements in solidarity with Palestinians. In mid-2009, the School of Oriental and African Studies (SOAS) organised another occupation, this time over the arrest and deportation of cleaning staff by the UK Border Agency. But the recent wave of occupations over fees and cuts was different. These occupations were taking place in the midst of a financial crisis in which the new government insisted that everyone had to pay, students included. This involved the tripling of tuition fees, the scrapping of the Education Maintenance Allowance (EMA), and up to 100 per cent cuts in government funding for arts and humanities subjects. For students, the immediate fight was about cuts to education but the movement quickly began making broader and more ambitious demands: free education, an end to the war in Afghanistan, scrapping Trident, and opposition to all cuts. This was reflected in the hundreds of homemade placards students brought to the demonstrations. Far from being a defensive or 'single-issue' movement, as some commentators suggested, arguments were being made against the spending priorities of the ConDem government. The occupations provided the forums for this politicisation and directed student anger into collective action.

By most accounts there were 46 occupations across the country at the end of 2010, the greatest show of militancy by students in a generation. For many, there was a recognition early on that university managements were going to get behind the government over cuts and fee increases, and so while the mass demonstrations focused anger at the government, the occupations directed this anger towards management at individual universities. The point was to put pressure on university administrations in order that they direct pressure against the government. The fight against both government and management was necessary, and it was the occupations that brought students – and eventually many staff – into direct confrontation with increasingly demoralised university principle-officers and vice-chancellors.

INSIDE THE OCCUPATIONS

Every university that went into occupation had their own process of debate and discussion, from securing a space to negotiating demands. The SOAS occupation came out of a packed emergency general meeting about how to respond to the cuts and tuition fee increases. There was fierce debate over whether to occupy, and the decision in favour was won by a mere eight votes. The democratic origins of the occupation proved important: once inside the occupation, every major decision was the result of an attempt to achieve consensus, and where that was not possible occupiers voted.

The demands of several of the occupations reflected both ambition – tempered with a sense of what was possible – and optimism. While some demands focused on pressuring university management publicly to condemn plans to raise fees and cut budgets, others were about pressuring management to refuse to implement fees and cuts altogether. Still others were about increasing financial transparency, reversing outsourcing policies and ensuring there were no staff redundancies. Most occupations also included the demand for occupiers or supporters not to be victimised for occupying or visiting the occupation. This was essential if the occupations were to mobilise students who were still unsure about its merits, and it facilitated a breadth of support that allowed many occupations to shed any reputation of being led only by the far left. Hundreds of students and staff came in and out of the occupations at most universities, either to attend tutorials or teach-ins or simply to show solidarity.

The reality was that students in occupation were taking risks. The threat of being disciplined by management was always there; there was also the threat of arrest by the bailiffs or the police; and of course the threat of serious disruption to their studies, given all the time spent away from studying. Everyone had something to worry about. So it was understandable that part of the aim was to gather support and numbers in order to minimise these risks. When the SOAS occupation was issued with a high court injunction, later reduced to a possession order, and management advised staff not to visit the occupation, the occupiers called an emergency staff and student meeting in the occupation space. There was intense discussion about whether to continue the occupation and on what basis. But in the context of growing public sentiment against fee increases, the mounting number of occupations, the looming vote in parliament, and the anger at the government, there was little choice. The vote to continue the occupation was unanimous.

A number of university management, together with others who disagreed with the occupations, portrayed them as immature and illegitimate forms of protest. The opposite was true. The general level of organisation inside the occupations was high, with schedules of activities laid out days in advance, teams of people allocated to specific tasks and lists of duties pinned to the walls inside the occupations, from cleaning the space to coordinating legal work. Crucially, it was inside the occupations where much of the organising for the demonstrations in late 2010 took place: providing stewards, printing leaflets, making banners, organising flashmobs in the run-up and mobilising students and staff across campuses. The size and breadth of the demonstrations once again put management on the back foot and clamping down on individual occupations became increasingly untenable.

The occupations were also forums where creativity and technical savvy could flourish. Occupations such as that at University College London (UCL) were examples to some of the others, with their colossal tweeting record and ability to develop software that enabled new forms of resistance. The mobile phone application Sukey, although it was developed after the major demonstrations, was designed to keep protesters informed of trouble spots and potential kettles during demonstrations. It was just one example of technological self-organisation; it almost goes without saying that Facebook, Twitter and blogs were the core organising tools for both the demonstrations and occupations. Old-fashioned text messaging was also key to informing occupiers and supporters of events, meetings and emergencies.

Occupations lasted anywhere from a few hours or days to several weeks. SOAS occupied on 22 November, and was among the first universities to occupy. Within 48 hours, 16 more universities had occupied. And more and more were planning occupations. Much of the initial media focus, however, remained on the broken windows at Millbank following the 10 November protest. The demonstrations that followed – on 24 and 30 November – gave further boosts to the occupations, where this time students as young as 13 were coming out against increased fees and the scrapping of EMA. By the time the last major demonstration was organised, on the day of the vote in parliament, SOAS and other occupations began thinking about how to end the occupations. The rationale was simple: rather than grow too tired to go on or lose sight of the reasons for occupying in the first place, it was essential that occupations were brought to an end on the occupiers' own terms. At SOAS it was 13 December, exactly three weeks after it began. A rally was held outside the occupation space, where speeches were made and slogans chanted. Staff and students watched and cheered as occupiers came out with their possessions.

WHAT THE OCCUPATIONS ACHIEVED

The immediate effect of the occupations was that they localised and polarised the debate within each university in a way that the demonstrations alone could never do. They served to turn passive agreement into active support. But were demands met? Not in the way that students would have wanted, because most occupations were effectively arguing for a reversal of planned cuts and fee increases. This was the main demand at SOAS. The other main demand was that management release a statement condemning planned tuition fee increases and call on vice-chancellors across the country to unite against threats to higher education. No such statement was made, but towards the end of the occupation a large proportion of SOAS staff had signed a letter to Paul Webley, SOAS vice-chancellor, condemning cuts and fee increases and expressing 'strong support' for the SOAS occupation.

The management at SOAS had already made it clear that school policy did not recognise occupations as a legitimate form of protest. People were confronted with a stark decision: do we support the occupation anyway or do we defend the management position that the cuts are inevitable? What if the occupation escalates? What if management are heavy-handed? Four days into the occupation and the entire school was talking about it. It was easier for the students to show support; they clearly had less to lose. For staff, however, it meant siding against their employers. Many took a 'wait and see' approach and there were deep divisions amongst the staff, at least initially. But by the second week, when SOAS management threatened to send in bailiffs, and more universities were occupying, a certain sense of pride about the occupation had surfaced. Students now had the moral high ground, and lecturers and support staff became vital to maintaining it. The lecturers helped organise teach-ins and teach-outs (impromptu lectures in nearby public spaces), support staff brought food for the occupiers, and union officials offered to stay awake all night on security rotas when the occupation was threatened with eviction. By this time it was clear that management policy prohibiting occupations had become meaningless.

But the occupations also helped bring the education debate to the rest of society. Should the students be supported in their increasingly confrontational battle to defend education or should the government be supported in its task to bring down the deficit? What kind of weight did the student movement have behind it? Was it possible for the students to force the government to reverse its plans? If the movement could unsettle the government, the whole logic of the ConDem ideology could be exposed for what it is: an attempt to uphold Britain as a global financial centre at the expense of the welfare state. Bringing the education debate to the centre of public attention inevitably opened up arguments against the cuts more generally. This was not accidental. Students were setting an example for workers inside and outside the university: if you support the occupations and the defence of education, what are you going to do when your workplace or library or local council is threatened with cuts? Waiting for official action could mean putting up no resistance at all.

It was the combination of official action – the demonstration called by NUS and UCU that kickstarted the movement – and unofficial action, reflected in the size and breadth of the occupations, that was the driving force behind the movement. The occupations were central forums in which unofficial action could develop because they were a source of constant polemic against *neoliberal* education: the underlying ethos was the idea of a free education zone, which was about creative thinking, alternative ideas and, crucially, a rejection of the marketisation of education. And the connections were made concrete. The flashmobs at Top Shop and Vodafone were about 'educating the market' while the teach-outs in busy train stations were about bringing free education to the public. The rejection of neoliberal education was for many students a rejection of neoliberalism itself.

This radicalisation in turn exposed the limits and weaknesses of the official leadership of the student movement, the NUS. One particularly revealing example was during the UCL occupation when NUS President Aaron Porter publicly apologised for being 'spineless and dithering' and promised not only to provide 'financial, legal and political aid' to the occupations, but also to call a demonstration on the day of the tuition fees vote. Within days Porter backtracked. The promise of a demonstration turned into a promise for a glowstick vigil, supported by the UCU, and attended by a few hundred people. In contrast, unofficial and non-traditional leaders were stepping up to lead the movement. The University of London Union (ULU), backed by the newly constituted London Student Assembly (LSA), together with the National Campaign Against Fees and Cuts (NCAFC) and Education Activist Network (EAN), called the demonstrations that the NUS failed to call. On 9 December 2010 over 30,000 students marched. It was clear that while the initial NUS demonstration on 10 November was hugely important because it mobilised on a broad scale and provided the backdrop to the occupations, the official leadership was incapable of fully reflecting student anger and intensifying the movement. The movement had already gone further than the NUS wanted, and yet there was a pressing need for an alternative leadership. The ULU, with its popular and fiery leader, Clare Solomon, was increasingly seen as this alternative.

There was much debate within the student movement and inside the occupations about leadership, including both the need for it and the dangers of leaders taking over the movement and diluting its creativity, radicalism and breadth. Many were of the opinion that this was a 'leaderless' movement. In truth the movement produced all kinds of leaders, including those that had never been involved in politics before. The SOAS occupation would not have happened if a group of students had not argued for occupation in the emergency general meeting in the first place. And it was precisely the initiative that students took to organising within the occupations that allowed the best occupations to grow and involve increasingly larger numbers of students. Without a level of organisation, led by people taking initiatives to a wider group, it would not have been possible to draw in large numbers of staff and students. Organisation meant that people were actually taking a lead, whether it was volunteering to negotiate with management or coordinating an event within the occupation space, and the success of the occupations depended directly on whether students were willing to take leadership roles. This leadership, in fact, portrayed the occupations as open and accountable spaces. In practice, all mass movements have leaderships, however shifting and fluid.

One of the most inspiring consequences of the success of the occupations was the effect it had on FE and school students. For many young people this was the first time they had come out on the streets to demonstrate. Many of them had already made the links: cuts to EMA and universities were part of a wider attack by the ConDem government on the people who can least afford to pay. Not only that, it was seen as a direct attack on young people. The political lessons were short and sharp. There was at least one sit-in at Camden High School for Girls and others were contemplating the possibilities, describing the movement as the fight for 'something far bigger'. The effects of this radicalisation will take time to materialise but what did happen is that tens of thousands of young people were asking fundamental questions about society: the neutrality of the police and the media, who has access to education and the best jobs, and the nature of parliamentary democracy.

THE FUTURE OF STUDENT RESISTANCE

The first London Student Assembly meetings after the Christmas 2010 holidays were crucial to sustaining the political debate generated during the occupations. They were big and positive, and the mood was still determined, despite the result of the vote in parliament and the end of all but one or two of the occupations. The student movement itself was conscious of what it had been able to achieve, splitting the Liberal Democrats, getting six Tory MPs to vote against their own bill, and raising the possibility of a national confrontation with the government over austerity measures.

But it is also true that the movement suffered a setback with the passing of the bill. The question is whether the subsequent post-holiday lull is only temporary. The effect of the vote on the wider student population cannot be underestimated, but the situation was also exacerbated by the left itself, which started to cut itself off from this wider movement. One of the most revealing examples was calling for a second demonstration in London after the NUS, backed by the TUC, called a demonstration in Manchester on 29 January. Instead of having one, united, mass demonstration in Manchester, led by the NUS, two relatively small demonstrations created a sense of division and a general lack of direction. Student leaders need to re-establish that connection with the wider movement. And this has to be done by focusing on opposing the government, not an obsession with the failings of the NUS. While it is true that Aaron Porter had attacked his own members and been weak and indecisive, the movement must be clear that he is not the main enemy.

The strategy for the future must be twofold: first to continue to build on the gains of the student movement and to make future education protests bigger and broader, through the hard and patient work of building student assemblies, engaging in union meetings and so forth; and second to reorient the movement towards building and inspiring the wider anti-cuts movement. It is entirely plausible that we could see another wave of occupations over solidarity with the revolutions of February 2011 in the Middle East or in protest at the closure of hundreds of libraries: occupations are now part of the tradition of the student movement in Britain, and can be reignited. Engaging with the wider anti-cuts movement provides the best hope of bringing back the hundreds of thousands of students who marched on the streets and made occupation a legitimate form of protest.

13

Achievements and Limitations of the UK Student Movement

Ashok Kumar[1]

In recent years, seemingly disparate struggles have broken out on university campuses across the world. The common thread is a resistance to the attacks on university education through cuts in state funding, but I shall argue that the fight back against neoliberal reforms should be understood as more than just a defence of the status quo.

For students in the UK who engaged in some of the fiercest protests in recent British history, the time to reflect is only now beginning. What started out as a response to education cuts has transformed into a more profound debate about the purpose of education under capitalism. This critique sees universities as preparation for a life of wage-labour and therefore as a system that reproduces existing inequalities and yet it would seem that student demonstrators were defending it. To what extent did the demonstrations and occupations constitute a radical critique of education itself or was the movement more limited in its demands?

Like the mass anti-war movement of 2003, the student movement of 2010 lost its immediate battle. Explaining why we lost is critical, not only to the continuation of the UK student movement, but to all progressive movements for change in the UK.

THE GLOBAL RESPONSE TO EDUCATION 'REFORM'

Cuts in public spending on education, the introduction of tuition fees and subsequent fee increases have become a common occurrence across the West, with widespread acceptance of this political 'reality'. In the USA, universities that charge substantial tuition fees are portrayed by those who run them as the optimal HE funding model. Australia re-introduced tuition fees in 1989, while seven out of 16 federal states in Germany introduced tuition fees in 2007. In Puerto Rico the government announced a 100 per cent tuition fee hike, the privatisation of higher education and $2 billion in cuts in 2009, a figure that translated into 30,000 lost jobs.

Anti-capitalist ideology aside, European and US student and trade union organisations are united in criticising what they perceive to be a shift in the burden of funding from the state to the individual in a way that seems irreversible. They are equally opposed to the way in which students are increasingly defined as consumers and as champions of 'choice' who use their 'buying power' to make an 'investment' in their future by choosing the university that most appeals to them. Students are now assumed to make decisions about their subject and university based on average graduate earnings, graduation job prospects and 'additional benefits' of the institution alone, and not because the student feels passionate, inspired or intrigued by a subject area.

Student responses to these changes have varied but can be broadly categorised in three groups: one group who actually support the changes, a second who are opposed to specific changes but who believe in an evolutionary approach to social change; and finally a group who oppose the changes but who believe in a more militant and revolutionary approach to social change. Although there is some crossover in the demands, beliefs and tactics between the latter two groups, those who make the link between a different kind of education and a different kind of society have employed a wide variety of tactics including occupations, sit-ins, repeated and impromptu demonstrations and, critically, have made demands that go beyond resisting the cuts. It is this group of students who have been successful in stopping course closures and departmental sell-offs. While largely defensive resistance to cuts through mass demonstrations and occupations has been able to mobilise students and express dissent, student strikes have proven more successful as a means of challenging systemic processes.

Recently, student strikes have sprung up in places as divergent as California and South Africa in opposition to austerity measures. Puerto Rico was met immediately with mass demonstrations of students and education workers. When these marches did little to dent the government's confidence, students then adopted a variety of methods in order to escalate the political fight. The General Assembly at the University of Puerto Rico (UPR), held by the Students' Union in April 2010, finally initiated an indefinite strike, which spread to all other UPR universities and only ended, 60 days later, as a result of the government's concessions to hold off on fee increases and privatisation. During the strike students had garnered support from teaching unions, national unions of university maintenance workers, as well as academic staff unions asking their members to respect all student picket lines.

In the Canadian province of Quebec, students marched against the government's plans too, but similarly made no progress in their negotiations. By February 2005 student unions in Montreal, mostly in francophone CEGEPs (similar to Further Education colleges in the UK), were calling for strike action. By mid-March, 230,000 students – more than half the students in Quebec – were on strike. By April, the government had not only acquiesced to student demands to reverse the planned cuts, but agreed to add an additional \$70 million for 2005–6.

In these instances, strikes were prompted by coordinated action around a united demand, founded through direct democratic processes – such as mass assemblies – which was a critical feature lacking in the UK. Although the French and Italian student movements have widely served as an inspiration, activists in the UK have hesitated about taking such radical measures, and have lacked a common constructive idea of how to reshape the education system. This may be related to the fact that the National Union of Students (NUS) has long been seen as the only 'legitimate' and 'democratic' body for students in the UK.

NUS AND THE MOVEMENT

The divide between the NUS and 'the movement' illustrates a clear rejection of the neoliberal consensus. In order to understand the NUS, we must first appreciate the role it played during more than a decade of New Labour-led austerity in which every increase in fees was met with the bare minimum of NUS tokenistic resistance.

The recent history of NUS national demonstrations reads like an ancient Greek tragedy. Fees are raised, students protest, nothing happens, students go home. Grants are abolished, students protest, nothing happens, students go home. With new injustices burdened upon the shoulders of incoming students, students have often mobilised but, lacking momentum and leadership, this mobilisation is quickly lost and the movement falters. Like Sisyphus forever rolling his boulder up a hill, student energies are often expended without significant gains. In many circumstances, as in the 2004 campaign against higher tuition fees, the battle appeared to have been lost by just a few votes in parliament. In reality however, it was the failure to build from protest and demonstrations something bigger and more serious that ensured the defeat of student struggles. The NUS has seven million members, but it also has a deep cultural inability to engage or mobilise its membership into something tangible. At best, it postures a ritual of outrage, before admitting defeat.

Many of the NUS's problems with mobilisation mirror those of the Labour Party. Like Labour, the NUS has overseen a monumental decline in grassroots activism as its politics have moved towards the centre. The language its leaders speak is the same language that the Blairites perfected concerning the need to 'modernise'. Its decision to move towards a form of graduate tax has bemused students everywhere – accepting fees in all but name and surrendering ground with no apparent advantage – and has failed to influence policy, with the exclusion of the NUS from the Browne report.

While the political core of the NUS was being eroded, a wave of governance restructurings changed the landscape of the student movement. The new corporate model, with its inclusion of external trustees – often business and university heads – in the most powerful union bodies, has instituted a culture that is fundamentally opposed to grassroots organisation. In recent years, the NUS has positioned itself as a national level lobbying group, with local unions as service providers, members as consumers, and democracy as expendable. Some unions no longer even have general meetings and the leadership of the student movement has spiralled away from the activists who used to sustain it. Under Labour, the NUS was quite happy to avoid mass national mobilisation. Under a Conservative government, however, these contradictions were at last brought into sharp focus.

On 10 November 2010, it was mainly the hastiness of the NUS's president to condemn the thousands of students who protested outside (and inside) Millbank, the headquarters of the ruling Conservatives, that was met with widespread criticism even among its own members. The NUS was perceived to have prioritised property damage over the anger of students caused by the intransigence of the political elite and the hypocrisy of the Liberal Democrats, who had pledged not to raise fees once in power. The strained efforts by the NUS to distance itself from 'a tiny minority' of students starkly resembled the government's efforts to drive a wedge between different factions of the opposition.

Contrary to the NUS's response to 10 November, the images of the occupation of Millbank Tower sent a clear message to those in power while allowing students to realize that, now, anything was possible. On the back of Millbank, two weeks later, some 130,000 students marched out of further education colleges across the country, while tens of thousands marched on 30 November and again on the day of the vote in Parliament on 9 December. Due to the lack of central organisation, activists quickly shifted to different kinds of operating platforms which were at first provided by other organisations that had built around the issues of fees and cuts. These included the Education Activist Network (EAN) and the National Campaign Against

Fees and Cuts (NCAFC) and the Coalition of Resistance which provided links between the student movement, pensioners, trade unions and other sections of society.

These organisations were rapidly complemented by the occupation of dozens of universities which became hubs of campus mobilisation. As we saw in the previous chapter, the occupations became a fertile ground for organising students who themselves learnt organising tactics through the daily struggle to retain the occupied spaces against potential police or university intervention. Shortly after the first occupation at SOAS, the London Student Assembly (LSA) was initiated to connect occupations in London more effectively and was followed by a National Student Assembly. Despite attempts to centralise the movement in London and elect representatives for the LSA, its direct democratic structure was maintained, true to the non-hierarchical spirit of the movement. Failing to grasp this, politicians and journalists searched in vain for the 'leaders' of the movement highlighting their inability to envision human beings showing independent initiative and self-organisation by means of participatory democracy.

The widespread dissatisfaction with the NUS on many campuses cut deeper than questioning the integrity of the NUS's democratic decision-making structures, with all eyes looking towards the actions and comments of the NUS president, Aaron Porter. Students grew increasingly tired of the NUS's inability to keep up with the 'movement' that had galloped ahead of it. While the movement called for over half a dozen forms of direct action over several months, the NUS leadership refused to back all but one in the name of preserving its precious reputation against so-called 'student thugs'. At different junctures, the movement spoke up: some student unions called for 'no confidence' motions, others gave him a frosty reception at campus visits, and many winced at the prospect of Aaron Porter running for a second term. This mood of dissatisfaction was proved by his decision not to stand for another term, the first time for a NUS president since 1969; the 'real' student movement had spoken and the NUS had finally listened.

DOES THE MOVEMENT IN THE UK HAVE A VISION?

The shift in NUS policy from free education paid through progressive taxation to a New Labour-backed graduate tax has had the benefit of consolidating politically disparate left-wing factions around a principled and united stand for education as a right. In addition, the consensus of the movement is a sound rejection both of government austerity measures and, with it, the NUS bureaucracy as the vehicle through which to resist. It is largely this 'anti-stance' that has tied the movement together. Most activists agree in their objection to the prioritisation of 'useful' or profitable STEM subjects while stripping the arts, humanities and social sciences of the entirety of their teaching grant. Activists also want to prevent the education system being stripped of most of its public funding in order to create an education market that would leave generations of young people with life-long, mortgage-sized debts. The explosion of student resistance at the tail-end of 2010 tells us that young people in the UK reject the ideological narratives being peddled as inevitable by those in power.

It is important to note that when fees were introduced in the UK in 1998, and subsequently increased in 2004 and 2010, they did not affect those already attending university. Unlike other countries that instituted fees, UK fees always remain fixed at the rate a student paid when they first started university. Thus, the organising for the first national demonstration was based on a collective defence of higher education and not around the self-interest of students themselves.

Beyond that, however, in lieu of structural unity, the various groups and factions that make up the student movement have had a series of disparate targets, messages and demands. The two main groups in the student movement, the EAN and NCAFC, have successfully called national demonstrations and yet the politics behind those calling for these successive 'Day Xs' seem removed from those who marched, occupied and battled the police on streets, town halls and campuses up and down the country. The highly publicised 'national convention' of the NCAFC, or the 'national education assembly' held by the

EAN, have been unable to attract more that 200 students, while demonstrations called by the same groups have brought out over 100,000 students onto the streets. So while it is undeniable that they have been able to call thousands into action at a week's notice, it is more difficult to say that these organisations are speaking for the movement.

In contrast to those nationwide organisations, most occupations focused their demands at the university level, for example, asking university vice-chancellors to release statements in opposition to the government's proposals, for a living wage for all workers on campus (if not already implemented), and for no victimisation of participants in the occupation.

Although the external narrative of the occupations highlighted the transitional demands to vice-chancellors, students used the occupations as a means of envisioning a new education. Leeds occupiers hosted a 're-imagining the university' conference, the University of the West of England's 'camp for education' included calling for 'inventing something better together', while many others proclaimed their occupations as 'a space for free thought and learning' – a clear message of what is currently missing from the university. As one UCL occupier put it: 'the occupations serve as a fast-track apprenticeship for activism' and, as we witnessed at LSE, the occupations became the seed for how students wanted their education to be.

After the vote in parliament on 9 December 2010, almost all the occupations were suspended. The movement thus lost a huge part of its grassroots foundation and its local democracy which, in conjunction with the lack of a unifying vision, severely curbed students in the New Year. Even though we have recently witnessed a revival of occupations – including those at Manchester, Royal Holloway, UCL and the LSE, where a 24-hour occupation led to a victory of nearly all our demands to force the university to refund all its donations from Gaddafi to the people of Libya – these occupations have had a short life expectancy. Indeed, some targets for occupation, like the University of London Union, a space already controlled by the left, show the divisive and confused direction some forces find themselves in.

As a consequence, many student activists have turned to new platforms of engagement, in search of a political vision. UK Uncut, for example, targets a broader range of institutions than government alone, including corporate tax-avoiders such as Vodaphone, Topshop and Boots, and has very effectively highlighted the reality of the cuts as ideological rather than economically necessary. The populist demand of 'pay your taxes', combined with opposition to bank bonuses, has forced the issue of corporate–government collusion on to media agendas and has helped to present a genuine alternative to cuts in the public sector. UK Uncut has broadened the debate on cuts, highlighted injustices, and allowed for autonomous self-organisation. Through insisting that their decisions are made 'through Twitter', the group can be seen as a highly autonomous and constructive continuation of the form of activism that defined the student movement of 2010. In recent days, however, the organisation has become a case study of what the 'tyranny of structurelessness' looks like when actualised. The lack of transparency has meant a highly mobile, secretive and effective network, but, at the same time, one that plays out the existing white, male, power structure in its self-appointed leaders.

Other groups went further in advancing a more coherent anti-capitalist message and questioning the notion of education as we know it today. Although they cannot be said to constitute 'the movement', such attempts to envision a genuinely alternative education have come from the ('Really') Free Schools (not to be confused with David Cameron's free schools) such as the Really Open University in Leeds, the LSE Free School and the Really Free School in London. The Free Schools see themselves as a space to question the structures of traditional education, to uncover the kind of world view it tacitly or openly represents, and attempts to furnish every participant with an equal say.

The London Really Free School marks a further convergence of student activists with a generally more alternative political milieu that draws its input from squatters, artists, climate camp activists, ideologically unorthodox autonomists and many others. The school can be seen as a nodal point of free, participatory education and public acquisition of fallow property, as well as creating open spaces at the heart of an ever more gentrified and marginalising metropolis. It is in this spirit that the Really Free School has changed its location three times since its first appearance in Bloomsbury, close to the British Museum. Its most recent house moving turned into a street carnival, stretching from the house from which it had been evicted in Fitzrovia to its new home – an ex-pub near Oxford Street.

CONCLUSION

Our generation is meant to be an example of unparalleled self-perceived impotence and depoliticisation. Its seminal moment, the Iraq war, saw the biggest wave of protest in British history and a unified demand, while the student demonstrations of today have witnessed some of the biggest student protests in UK history. Both have experienced a clear refusal by government to consider our demands. What movements such as these achieved were not concrete wins but an ingrained frustration amongst a growing and mobilised section of young people. In fighting for the heart and soul of education, we may redefine what it means to resist. The students who took to the streets were not defending the education factories we so resent, but were fighting back against education becoming more of what it already is.

The failure of this movement has been its inability to reflect and articulate the problems with the existing education system and the wider socio-economic system. This failure is not a failure of ordinary students who, I have argued, managed to make links between their demands and wider society. In focusing the 'fightback' exclusively on the cuts, the movement's traditional leadership failed adequately to critique the existing system. It is tempting to suggest that we almost made it: a demo that exceeded turnout expectations by 40,000 which was then overshadowed by the NUS's condemnation of the Millbank violence. But the movement must recognise that the marketisation of higher education in the UK happened long before the financial crisis, long before this Tory–Lib Dem government and long before the subsequent drive for austerity.

As the recent battles come to a close, new structures of resistance are coming to terms with the failure of the movement to draft an alternative to the existing system. The appearance of Free Schools in Bloomsbury and the LSE, which are actively fighting the cuts and retaining a radical critique of a commodified education system, provide one such alternative. Let us hope that the energy and militancy of the movement throw up others that are able to unite students in campaigns to build the kinds of universities we need.

NOTE

1. With contributions from Jakob Schaefer.

Part V

International Perspectives

14

Beyond the Swindle of the Corporate University

Henry A. Giroux

In spite of being discredited by the economic recession of 2008, neoliberalism, or market fundamentalism as it is called in some quarters, has once again returned with a vengeance. The Gilded Age has come back, with big profits for the rich and increasing impoverishment and misery for the middle and working classes. Political illiteracy has cornered the market on populist rage, providing a political bonus for those who are responsible for massive levels of inequality, poverty and sundry other hardships. As social protections are dismantled, public servants are denigrated and public goods such as schools, bridges, health care services and public transportation deteriorate, the Obama administration unapologetically embraces the values of economic Darwinism and rewards its chief beneficiaries: mega banks and big business. Neoliberalism – reinvigorated by the passing of tax cuts for the ultra rich, the right-wing Republican Party taking over of the House of Representatives, and an ongoing successful attack on the welfare state – proceeds once again in zombie-like fashion to impose its values, social relations, and forms of social death upon all aspects of civic life.[1]

With its relentless attempts to normalise the irrational belief in the ability of markets to solve all social problems, neoliberal market fundamentalism puts in place policies designed to dismantle the few remaining vestiges of the social state and vital public services. More profoundly, it has weakened if not nearly destroyed those institutions that enable the production of a formative culture in which individuals learn to think critically, imagine other ways of being and doing, and connect their personal troubles with public concerns. Matters of justice, ethics and equality have once again been exiled to the margins of politics. Never has this assault on the democratic polity been more obvious, if not more dangerous, than at the current moment, when a battle is being waged under the rubric of neoliberal austerity measures on the autonomy of academic labour, the classroom as a site of critical pedagogy, the rights of students to high quality education, the democratic vitality of the university as a public sphere and the role played by the liberal arts and humanities in fostering an educational culture that is about the practice of freedom and mutual empowerment.[2]

While higher education has a long history of being attacked by various religious, political and corporate forces, there is something unique about the current assault on the university.[3] At various points in the past, such as during the McCarthy era, individual professors were assailed for their political beliefs and affiliations.[4] During the 1980s and 1990s, progressive academics were initially targeted for their critical views toward the canon and for allegedly indoctrinating students.[5] They were seen as a threat by various right-wing ideologues and corporate groups who never forgot the challenge posed by student radicals of the 1960s to the increasing corporatisation and militarisation of the university.[6] While the relationship of the university to corporate power and the warfare state was never far removed from the workings of the university, its hidden order of politics was partially offset by a democratic legacy, set of liberal ideals and a commitment to public values that strongly resonated with America's claim on the principles of democracy.[7] The institutional setting provided a space for the nurturing of democratic ideals, and offered both a shelter for radical intellectuals and a mode of critique that vigorously defended higher education's public role and the formative culture and modes of literacy that were essential to its survival and promise.[8] Such a democratic mandate for the university, however compromised at times, was emboldened by various struggles for racial, gender, economic and social justice in the second half of the twentieth century. The culture that made such struggles possible offered more than opportunities for political alignments. It also reinforced the long-standing view of the university as a democratic public sphere. Within such a sphere, critique, dialogue, critical theory and informed judgment constituted a pedagogical necessity through which the institution could develop a public awareness of itself and empower administrators, researchers, teachers and students to act in socially responsible ways that made such an awareness meaningful to those both inside and outside of the university.

As a result of this enduring, though tarnished, historical narrative, the democratic expression of pedagogical diversity and the political nature of education were viewed by many members of the American public and intellectual classes as central not only to the civic mission of the university, especially the humanities and liberal arts, but also to the functioning of a just and democratic society. We are reminded of this legacy in recent times by Jacques Derrida's Enlightenment notion of the university as a place to think, to ask questions, and to exercise the autonomy necessary to both challenge authority and make it accountable.[9] However, under the onslaught of a merciless economic Darwinism and theatre of cruelty that has emerged since the 1980s, the historical legacy of the university as a vital public good no longer fits into a revamped discourse of progress in which the end goal is narrowed to individual survival rather than the betterment of society as a whole. In fact, the concept of social progress has all but disappeared amid the ideological discourse of a crude market-driven presentism that has a proclivity for instant gratification, consumption and immediate financial gain.

Memories of the university as a citadel of democratic learning have been replaced by a university eager to define itself largely in economic terms. For instance, Thomas College, a liberal arts school in Maine, advertises itself as 'the home of the Guaranteed Job!'[10] At Texas A&M University, faculty evaluations are based on three key pieces of information: 'their salary, how much external research funding they received and how much money they generated from teaching'.[11] According to university administrators, 'The information will allow officials to add the funds generated by a faculty member for teaching and research and subtract that sum from the faculty member's salary'[12] as the sole measure of faculty performance. In this entrepreneurial logic, if the faculty member does not produce more wealth than he or she is paid, their performance is devalued. Surely, this type of thinking could only be hatched in some conservative think-tank eager to relegate all faculty to the status of Wal-Mart workers. What is clear in this model of calculus of hyper-rationality is that quantity compensates for quality and pedagogy is freed from any notion of ethical and social responsibility.

Frank Ashley, the vice-chancellor for academic affairs at Texas A&M, justifies this conservative and corporate accountability model on the grounds that it proves to the people of Texas that academia 'pull[s] its weight.'[13] Chancellor Michael D. McKinney also relies on a consumerist approach by measuring good classroom teaching according to student satisfaction. McKinney rewards faculty by offering a $10,000 bonus to teachers who get the highest student evaluations. He justifies the approach by stating: 'This is customer satisfaction ... It has to do with students having the opportunity to recognize good teachers and reward them with some money.'[14] And yet the research is abundantly clear in concluding that student evaluations are unreliable indicators of teacher performance. Such an approach does no more than reinforce a neoliberal notion of students as customers paying for a service, turning faculty teaching into a form of entertainment that plays to what Cary Nelson, the president of the American Association of University Professors, calls 'the applause meter.'[15] Within this framework of simply giving students what they want, the notion of effective teaching as that which challenges commonsense assumptions and provokes independent, critical thought in ways that might be unsettling for some students as well as requiring from them hard work and introspection is completely undermined. Market-driven rewards cancel out the ethical imagination, social responsibility, and the pedagogical imperative of truth telling in favour of pandering to the predatory instincts of narrow-minded individual awards and satisfactions. This is the self-deception if not pedagogy of scoundrels.

As the centre of gravity shifts away from the humanities and the notion of the university as a public good, university presidents ignore public values while refusing to address major social issues and problems.[16] Instead, such administrators now display corporate affiliations like a badge of honour, sit on corporate boards and pull in huge salaries. Until recently, Ruth Simmons, the president of Brown University, sat on the board of Goldman Sachs and in 2009 earned $323,539 from the directorship and received a total of around $4.3 million in stock grants and options while serving on the board.[17] And she is not alone. A survey conducted by the *Chronicle of Higher Education* reported that '19 out of 40 presidents from the top 40 research universities sat on at least one company board'.[18] Rather than being treated as a social investment in the future, students are now viewed by university administrators as a major source of revenue for banks and other financial institutions that provide funds for them to meet escalating tuition payments. For older generations, higher education opened up opportunities for self-definition as well as pursuing a career in the field of one's choosing. It was relatively cheap, rigorous and accessible, even to many working-class youth. But as recent events in both the United States and Britain make clear, this is no longer the case. Instead of embodying the hope of a better life and future, higher education has become prohibitively expensive and exclusionary, now offering primarily a credential and for most students a lifetime of debt payments. Preparing the best and the brightest has given way to preparing what might be called Generation Debt.[19]

As the alleged golden age of higher education is mortgaged off to market-based values and instrumentalist modes of rationality, communal loyalties, deep-seated solidarities and long-term commitments are sacrificed to private interests, individual life pursuits and the new order of egoism.[20] As Sheldon Wolin has insightfully pointed out, the ideal of public commitment and the public spheres that sustain it have now become lost to history, fractured like public time itself by the frenetic speed at which financial transactions are exchanged, information is consumed, commitments are dissolved and marginalised subjects are rendered disposable. Historical amnesia now works in tandem with the accelerated pace of capital to loosen the connection between higher education and public values, and with it the connection between pedagogy as a moral and political practice and the formative culture necessary for substantive democracy.[21] Memory and loss now make an urgent claim upon theory to assert that which 'survives of the defeated, the indigestible, the unassimilated, the "cross grained", [and] the now wholly obsolete' and to become one of the few terrains left to imagine higher education beyond the corporate and militaristic logic of contemporary neoliberal values, politics and modes of governance.[22]

For the last three decades, we have witnessed in the United States the resurgence of a neoliberal disciplinary apparatus that has attempted to eradicate the social state, the concept of the public good and any trace of the social contract. The obligations of citizenship have been replaced by the demands of consumerism, education has been reduced to another market-driven sphere, pedagogy has been instrumentalised and public values have been transformed into private interests. Market values, culture and public pedagogy offer up a new understanding of the citizen as a consumer, the university as hostage to the imperatives of business culture, and academic labour as a new subaltern class engaged in the production of the next generation of neoliberal subjects. At the same time, we have witnessed the substitution of political sovereignty for economic sovereignty and the replacement of the social state with a punishing state defined by a survival-of-the-fittest ethic in which individuals now bear sole responsibility for their hardships, regardless of whether such forces are out of their reach and out of their control. As public issues collapse into private concerns, it becomes increasingly difficult to engage what C. Wright Mills called 'the sociological imagination', defined as the ability to relate individual actions to larger historical and relational totalities, to connect private issues to broader public considerations.[23] Under such circumstances, not only is the power of dissent depoliticised and weakened but those institutions and modes of thinking that embrace public values, democratic modes of critique and a commitment to social justice and social responsibility are either defined as nostalgic reminders of the past or viewed as dangerous threats to a market society that considers itself synonymous with democracy. Those modes of agency that might be used for structural change, for rejecting the fetishism of the market and reimagining social relations not tied to the obligations of consumerism and hyper-individualism, now appear increasingly out of place in the current historical moment.

The current assault threatening higher education cannot be understood outside of the crisis of public values, ethics, youth and democracy itself. This state of emergency must take as its starting point what Tony Judt has called 'the social question' with its emphasis on addressing acute social problems, providing social protections for the disadvantaged, developing public spheres aimed at promoting the collective good, and protecting educational spheres that enable and deepen the knowledge, skills and modes of agency necessary for a substantive democracy to flourish.[24] Putting the social question on the agenda for reclaiming higher education as a public good means encouraging progressives, students, artists, academics and others to examine those larger political, economic and cultural forces that undermine all vestiges of solidarity, disdain any viable notion of the social state, relegate all social protections to a form of pathology and assiduously work to destroy those public spheres that provide the formative culture necessary for the production of critical agents, civic courage and collective struggles against the myriad anti-democratic forces now threatening American society.

What is new about the current threat to higher education is the increasing pace of the corporatisation and militarisation of the university, the squelching of academic freedom, the rise of an ever increasing contingent of part-time faculty, and the view that students are basically consumers and faculty providers of a saleable commodity such as a credential or a set of workplace skills. More strikingly still is the slow death of the university as a centre of critique, vital source of civic education and crucial public good. Or, to put it more specifically, the consequence of such dramatic transformations has resulted in the near-death of the university as a democratic public sphere. Many faculty are now demoralised as they increasingly lose their rights and power. Moreover, a weak faculty translates into one governed by fear rather than by shared responsibilities and one that is susceptible to labour-bashing tactics such as increased workloads, the casualisation of labour and the growing suppression of dissent. Demoralization often translates less into moral outrage than into cynicism, accommodation and a retreat into a sterile form of professionalism. What is also new is that faculty now find themselves staring into an abyss, either unwilling to address the current attacks on the university or befuddled over how the language of specialisation and professionalisation has cut them off from not only connecting their work to larger civic issues and social problems but also developing any meaningful relationships to a larger democratic polity.

As faculty no longer feel compelled to address important political issues and social problems, they are less inclined to communicate with a larger public, uphold public values or engage in a type of scholarship that is available to a broader audience.[25] Beholden to corporate interests, career building and the insular discourses that accompany specialised scholarship, too many academics have become overly comfortable with the corporatisation of the university and the new regimes of neoliberal governance. Chasing after grants, promotions and conventional research outlets, many academics have retreated from larger public debates and refused to address urgent social problems. Assuming the role of the disinterested academic or the clever faculty star on the make, these so-called academic entrepreneurs simply reinforce the public's perception that they have become largely irrelevant. Incapable, if not unwilling, to defend the university as a democratic public sphere and a crucial site for learning how to think critically and act with civic courage, many academics have disappeared into a disciplinary apparatus that views the university not as a place to think but as a place to prepare students to be competitive in the global marketplace.

But higher education has a responsibility not only to search for the truth regardless of where it may lead, but also to educate students to make authority and power politically and morally accountable. Though questions regarding whether the university should serve *strictly* public rather than private interests no longer carry the weight of forceful criticism as they did in the past, such questions are still crucial in addressing the purpose of higher education and what it might mean to imagine the university's full participation in public life as the protector and promoter of democratic values. Indeed, higher education may be one of the few public spheres left where knowledge, values, and learning offer a glimpse of the promise of education for nurturing public values, critical hope and a substantive democracy. This is a particularly important insight in a society where not only the free circulation of ideas is being replaced by ideas managed by the dominant media but critical ideas are increasingly viewed or dismissed as banal, if not reactionary. Additionally, as neoliberal ideology is enlisted to narrow the parameters of the purpose of higher education, it increasingly limits – through high tuition rates, technocratic modes of learning, the reduction of faculty to temporary workers, and authoritarian modes of governance – the ability of many young people to attend college while at the same time refusing to provide a critical education to those who do. Hence the need for educators and young people to move beyond the language of critique and a discourse of both moral and political outrage, however necessary, to a sustained individual and collective defence of the university as a vital public sphere central to democracy itself.

Sadly, not enough faculty, students, parents and others concerned about the fate of young people and democracy are mobilising both in and outside of the university, willing and able to defend higher education as a public good and critical pedagogy as a moral and political practice that builds the capacity of young people to become engaged social agents. Under such circumstances, higher education, and especially the humanities, will enter a death spiral unlike anything we have seen in the past. Not even a shadow of its former self, the university will become simply another institution and vocational programme entirely at odds with imperatives of critical thought, dissent, social responsibility and civic courage. In fact, I think we can go further and suggest that we are at a turning point in American history in which what is at stake is not limited to the possibility of higher education as a public good but extends to the very possibility of enlightened literacy, politics and democracy itself. And that raises serious questions about what educators are going to do within the current historical climate to make sure that they do not succumb to the authoritarian forces circling the university, waiting for the resistance to stop and the lights to go out.

NOTES

1. Some useful sources on neoliberalism include: Lisa Duggan, *The Twilight of Equality* (Boston, MD: Beacon Press, 2003); David Harvey, *A Brief History of Neoliberalism* (New York: Oxford University Press, 2005); Wendy Brown, *Edgework: Critical Essays on Knowledge and Politics* (Princeton, NJ: Princeton University Press, 2005); Alfredo Saad-Filho and Deborah Johnston, (eds), *Neoliberalism: A Critical Reader* (London: Pluto Press, 2005); Neil Smith, *The Endgame of Globalization* (New York: Routledge, 2005); Aihwa Ong, *Neoliberalism as Exception: Mutations in Citizenship and Sovereignty* (Durham, NC: Duke University Press, 2006); Randy Martin, *An Empire of Indifference: American War and the Financial Logic of Risk Management* (Durham, NC: Duke University Press, 2007); Naomi Klein, *The Shock Doctrine: The Rise of Disaster Capitalism* (New York: Knopf, 2007); Henry A. Giroux, *Against the Terror of Neoliberalism* (Boulder, CO: Paradigm Publishers, 2008); David Harvey, *The Enigma of Capital and the Crisis of Capitalism* (New York: Oxford University Press, 2010); and Gerard Dumenil and Dominique Levy, *The Crisis of Neoliberalism* (Cambridge, MA: Harvard University Press, 2011).

2. See, for example, Stanley Aronowitz, *Against Schooling: For an Education That Matters* (Boulder: Paradigm Publishers, 2008); Christopher Newfield, *Unmaking the Public University* (Cambridge: Harvard University Press, 2008); and Ellen Schrecker, *The Lost Soul of Higher Education* (New York: New Press, 2010). One of the most extensive compilations analysing this assault can be found in Edward J. Carvalho and David B. Downing, (eds), *Academic Freedom in the Post-9-11 Era* (New York: Palgrave, 2010); and my forthcoming book, Henry A. Giroux, *Education and the Crisis of Public Values* (New York: Peter Lang Publishing, 2011).

3. I take this issue up in great detail in Henry A. Giroux, *The University in Chains: Confronting the Military-Industrial-Academic Complex* (Boulder, CO: Paradigm Publishers, 2008).

4. See, for example, Ellen Schrecker, *No Ivory Tower: McCarthyism and the Universities* (New York: Oxford University Press, 1986).

5. Classic examples would include Alan Bloom, *The Closing of the American Mind* (New York: Simon and Schuster, 1988); Charles Sykes, *Profscam: Professors and the Demise of Higher Education* (Washington, DC: Regnery Press, 1988); Thomas Sowell, *Inside American Education: The Decline, The Deception, The Dogmas* (New York: The Free Press, 1993) and Martin Anderson, *Imposters in the Temple* (New York: Simon and Schuster, 1992).

6. For a history of student resistance both within and outside the university, see Mark Edelman Boren, *Student Resistance: A History of the Unruly Subject* (New York: Routledge, 2001).

7. Ian Angus, *Love the Questions: University Education and Enlightenment* (Winnipeg, Canada: Arbeiter Ring Publishing, 2009).

8. This issue is taken up in great detail in Henry A. Giroux and Susan Searls Giroux, *Take Back Higher Education* (New York: Palgrave, 2004); and Susan Searls Giroux, *Between Race and Reason: Violence, Intellectual Responsibility, and the University to Come* (Stanford, CA: Stanford University Press, 2010).

9. See Jacques Derrida, 'The future of the profession or the university without condition (thanks to the 'humanities,' and what could take place tomorrow)', in Tom Cohen, (ed.), *Jacques Derrida and the Humanities: A Critical Reader* (Cambridge: Cambridge University Press, 2001), pp. 24–57.

10. Kate Zernike, 'Making college "relevant"', *New York Times* (3 January 2010), p. ED16.

11. Vimal Patel, 'A&M system grades faculty – by bottom line', *TheEagle.com* (1 September 2010). Online at: http://www.theeagle.com/am/A-amp-amp-M-grades-faculty

12. Ibid.

13. Ibid.

14. Scott Jaschik, 'Faculty pay "by applause Meter"', *Inside Higher Ed* (13 January 2009). Online at: http://www.insidehighered.com/news/2009/01/13/bonuspay

15. Ibid.

16. See Isabelle Bruno and Christopher Newfield, 'Can the Cognitariat Speak?' *E-Flux* No. 14 (March 2010). Online at: http://www.e-flux.com/journal/view/118/. See also Christopher Newfield, *Unmaking the Public University* (Cambridge, MA: Harvard University Press, 2008).

17. Graham Bowley, 'The Academic–Industrial Complex', *New York Times* (31 July 2010). Online at: http://query.nytimes.com/gst/fullpage.html?res=9E01EFDA143DF932A3575BC0A9669D8B63&ref=graham_bowley&pagewanted=4

18. Cited in ibid.

19. For an interesting critique of this issue, see the special issue of *The Nation* called 'Out of Reach: Is College Only for the Rich?' (29 June 2009).

20. Zygmunt Bauman, *Liquid Fear* (London: Polity Press, 2006).

21. For an interesting discussion of this issue, see Gayatri Chakravorty Spivak, 'Changing Reflexes: Interview with Gayatri Chakravorty Spivak,' *Works and Days* 55/56 (2010), pp. 1–21. I have also taken up this issue in a number of books. See most recently Henry A. Giroux, *Youth in a Suspect Society* (New York: Palgrave, 2009); and my forthcoming *Henry A. Giroux on Critical Pedagogy* (New York: Continuum Press, 2011).

22. Sheldon Wolin, 'Political Theory: From Vocation to Invocation', in Jason Frank and John Tambornino, (eds), *Vocations of Political Theory* (Minneapolis: University of Minnesota Press, 2000), p. 4.

23. C. Wright Mills, *The Sociological Imagination* (Oxford: Oxford University Press, 2000).

24. Tony Judt, *Ill Fares the Land* (New York: Penguin, 2010).

25. This argument has been made against academics for quite some time, although it has either been forgotten or conveniently ignored by many faculty. See, for example, various essays in C. Wright Mills, 'The powerless people: the role of the intellectual in society', in C. Wright Mills, *The Politics of Truth: Selected Writings of C. Wright Mills* (Oxford: Oxford University Press, 2008), pp. 13–24; Edward Said, *Humanism and Democratic Criticism* (New York: Columbia University Press, 2004); and Henry A. Giroux and Susan Searls Giroux, *Take Back Higher Education* (New York: Palgrave, 2004).

15
Education Reforms in a European Context[1]

Marion von Osten

You are a part of the most privileged ten percent of your generation, part of that minuscule group which has completed university studies. Public investment in each of you is fifteen times the educational investment in the average member of the poorest ten percent of the population, who drop out of school before completing the fifth grade. The certificate you receive today attests to the legitimacy of your competence. It is not available to the self-educated, to those who have acquired competence by means not officially recognized in Puerto Rico.[2]

Ivan Illich's celebrated comments to graduating doctoral students at the University of Puerto Rico in 1969 reflected a growing impatience with traditional concepts of education in Europe and North America. Illich's criticism had two pillars. One line of critique referred to a classical tradition in education that accepted school as an instrument to achieve social equality, which had been advocated as early as the eighteenth century by Pestalozzi and others. According to Illich, the introduction of compulsory school attendance had supported the bourgeois revolution in Europe and its former colonies and engendered a middle class freed from feudal dependencies. For certain groups of the population, the school system had furthered social mobility, enabling new professions and careers, particularly for men, in which they established relative autonomy vis-à-vis feudal power and new relations of capital. In the twentieth century, according to Illich, school was nothing more than a 'sacred cow', 'a central myth-making ritual'[3] of industrialised society. The emancipatory dynamism no longer existed because, on the one

157

hand, it had ceded to the ideologies and technocracies of learning and educating and, on the other, two-thirds of South American society had been excluded from educational institutions.

Moreover (as the second line of critique), he maintained that an educational paradox is inherent to school and university. Not everything that is part of the syllabus can also be called education while, at the same time, many abilities and competences gained outside school are not acknowledged as education by the institutions. Therefore, Illich evoked the possible end of the age of schooling, since the school system as a whole can no longer deny its counterproductive social effects. The institutional education system, he argued, produces nothing more than standardised formulas that help reproduce and reinforce the relations of rule and class not only in the decolonized spaces of Africa, Asia and South America but also in the wealthy industrialized world of the North.

THE GERMAN EDUCATION DISASTER

This was not the first crisis in education in the post-war period. After the Sputnik shock and in the wake of the first international innovation crisis in industrial production in Western Europe at the end of the 1950s, all political parties sought for the best educational reform so as to remain 'innovative'. In the Federal Republic of Germany (FRG) in the 1960s, educational policies were at the centre of public attention for an entire decade. After Georg Picht in 1964 had proclaimed 'the German education disaster',[4] all political parties in the FRG agreed that the 'utilisation of unutilized educational reserves' was the only possibility not to fall back behind the Eastern bloc in the competition for scientific innovation. The general aim was to increase participation in education, above all for those at a social disadvantage, and to transform the system of higher education in the FRG from the 'education of an elite to education of the masses'. Since the capacities of the existing universities had been exceeded, this targeted educational recruitment could be successfully implemented only through the establishment of new universities. Within two decades dozens of new universities, polytechnics and higher educational institutions were founded in Germany alone. They were popular with political parties and accepted enthusiastically by the public because they promised positively to accompany the structural change in industrialised society, which was confronted by an imminent crisis in production and sales of goods, as well as with demands for rights and higher wages by workers.

Thus, already in the early 1960s, the German, Humboldt-style universities model was called into question and demands for a division of the course of studies into basic studies and advanced studies were made. These demands were also advocated by the Verband Deutscher Studentenschaft (the Federation of German Students) in 1962 as well as by the Social Democrats, who additionally proposed to shorten the course of studies. But a structure of studies following the US model was rejected by professors at the time. They saw the ideal of the combination of research and teaching threatened and feared that the university would be transformed in a classical school which would reduce their own privileges. A few years later, in 1968, students protested against the implementation of this educational reform, since they presumed that elites would be selected in this process of hierarchization of studies, which was an obstacle to their goals for the democratisation of the university.

At the same time, the creation of new higher education institutes and polytechnics, in addition to the massive number of universities and their reform in the 1960s and 1970s, already constituted a compromise in the direction of a two-class system. Through targeted educational recruitment, the number of persons who had done the Abitur[5] had already increased significantly in the 1960s and 70s. The 1964 discourse on a state of emergency in education was followed by a comprehensive mobilisation of society to higher education and an increasingly positive judgment of knowledge-based, immaterial production vis-à-vis manual labour. This was a notion that, as it turned out, was also approved by those with different objectives. Private initiatives, such as the campaign 'Jugend Forscht' carried out for the first time in 1965 by the *Stern* magazine, contributed to creating an expressly male atmosphere of the origin-neutral 'highly intelligent schoolchild' accompanied by successful entre-preneurship. These pop-cultural strategies copied from American science fairs brought the direct application of scientific work for private enterprise into play and paved the way for the wide support, until today, of scientific and mathematical training and research considered necessary for business and trade. In early-1960s Germany, not only 'workers' children' were discovered as a knowledge resource and encouraged, as so-called educational reserves, to embark on a university career, but also technical professions deemed increasingly necessary were already marked out in school through the central role that mathematics and scientific subjects played.

THE REPRODUCTION OF CLASS POSITIONS

In the educational debates of the 1960s, the Italian and French left had taken on a radically different position, conceiving of school and factory, knowledge and labour, in a different way. They argued that the school system creates and perpetuates a hierarchy of engineers and workers and called for the development of new educational concepts and critical institutions in which workers were to receive the same amount of education as the children of the bourgeoisie, while at the same time fundamentally changing the contents conveyed at universities and schools. The experiences with workers' struggles and strikes in Italy and France led to the circulation of a new understanding of militant knowledge that not only criticised the knowledge produced in universities as that of dominance but regarded other forms of knowledge as valuable and value-creating.[6] The change consisted in recognising the benefits of knowledge which laborers gain at work and therefore including it in the curricula. This orientation towards practice was a way to counteract the social separation between manual work and brainwork. The practices themselves, whether manual labor on machines or political work in self-organisation, were acknowledged as central knowledge practices; collective experience and decision-making was set in opposition to the bourgeois concept of authorship. It was not only the demand for the integration of workers into the established knowledge apparatus but a fundamental change in the structure and method of knowledge and cultural production. This applied to the university, the factory, housing, schools, museums, art associations, and so on. In the 1970s, alternative and informal universities were also established, mainly arising from social movements such as the feminist movement that propagated other forms of conveying and appropriating knowledge.[7]

Hence, the demands of the late 1960s and early 1970s included, on the one hand, the classical motif that schools and universities must be freely accessible to all strata of society, since this had engendered social mobility, and on the other, that these educational institutions would guarantee a way to dissolve class barriers through the production of knowledge – during and after the course of education. Hope for social change was placed in schools and universities and to them was attributed not only a disciplinary but also an emancipatory and a socialist task. In the 1970s, colleges of education flourished; they were engaged not only in the critique of the bourgeois school, but also in drawing up alternative curricula and in project-related teaching, while recognising the knowledge acquired through manual labour, everyday and popular culture. One motif that can be repeatedly found in the 1970s is that everyday life and education must not be conceived separately but as intertwined. The culture of the teacher as all-knowing was called into question. And knowledge was produced everywhere: in the Fiat factory in Turin, in the Märkische Viertel district of Berlin, in the squats in Bologna, and on the streets and in the clubs of London.

Today, within the framework of populist debates on education ranging from Pisa to Bologna, a completely new 'spirit of education' can be observed that regards education no longer merely as the provision of a public resource but as a demand that the subjects of knowledge must renew on their own throughout their entire life. This applies not only to the increasing significance of certified school and university diplomas but also to social and cultural competences developed outside school. Whoever is not willing to do so or simply cannot achieve this lifelong update has not only done something wrong, but becomes a problem that is increasingly addressed in the media and by politics. The school system of institutionalised inequality is no longer called into question today but is instead stabilised through reforms. In this context, the notions of elite and excellence bear eloquent witness to a turn away from the concept of education for all to the legitimisation of segregation. Social groups that, for a variety of reasons, cannot or do not want to perform their intelligence and excellence according to these demands today not only drop out of the school system but are increasingly treated as an educational problem, something that is particularly the case for certain groups of youths, usually children from immigrant backgrounds.

THE BOLOGNA BUBBLE

The primary aim of the original Bologna Declaration in 1999 was to create a European area for higher education and research. However, what has emerged from the national implementation of the Bologna Declaration is that the implementation of these aims – such as mobility and the comparability of student performance and qualifications – often has the opposite effect to that intended. New hierarchies in university degrees, and thus in the labour market, have been introduced that contradict the goals of democratic education and employment policy.[8]

While the original Bologna Declaration envisaged trans-European degrees, it alludes only to the two-tier degree system that has accompanied the reforms as consecutive 'cycles' of education. The Austrian Ministry for Science and Research, in its report on the status of the implementation of the Bologna targets, also stated that the European reform process demanded the introduction of a system 'essentially based on two main cycles' as well as 'a system of credits such as the ECTS system' and a 'system of easily readable and comparable degrees'.[9] However in Switzerland, Germany and Austria, the Bologna process has been widely equated with the introduction of the BA and MA degrees. In Germany, the four- to five-year *Diplom* has been steadily abolished in favour of the three-year BA. Yet the Bologna Declaration and its successor agreements made no concrete suggestions in this regard. Because the Declaration is an EU directive, it can be duly interpreted and implemented only by national actors. These national interpretations have already led to an increasing heterogenisation of degrees within the EU so that ten years after the first Declaration, it is impossible to talk of homogenisation and greater comparability of education in the European area. Hence the headline of the *Frankfurter Allgemeine Zeitung* on 24 November 2009: 'Die Bologna Blase ist geplatzt' ('The Bologna bubble has burst').

However, one does need to distinguish between the Bologna documents, the praxis of the Bologna Process and the political use of the label 'Bologna' in the national context. The introduction of the two-tiered degree as planned in Austria results most significantly in a hierarchisation of university education that cannot immediately be inferred from the Bologna Declaration. The planned BA courses basically follow the logic of higher education as provided by a technical college – job-oriented, mid-level, applied – in new, modulated form. Now, however, this logic has been extended to degree courses formerly offered only in universities. Particularly in the recognition of degrees, the *Diplom* is now only valid as the first degree in the German-speaking space, although a *Diplom* together with a *Magister* continues to qualify the holder to go on to PhD and is more than equivalent to the two main cycles. The BA, on the other hand, is the first degree in the sense of a technical college (*Fachhochshule*) degree. Unlike the *Diplom*, the BA entitles only a minority of graduates to obtain an academic education (MA/PhD) in the narrower sense. In Austria, a BA qualifies its holder for no more than an upper-middle civil service position, while top-level positions, above all in research, are reserved for the minority of MA graduates.

In Scandinavia, a quota system had to be quickly abandoned when the BA failed on the labour market, while a resolution of the Conference of German Cultural Ministers on 15 October 2009 recognised criticisms from students about the 'schoolification' of university courses, the restrictive recognition of academic performance, the decrease in national and international mobility, the low acceptance of the BA as a professional qualification and the complicated credits system. In Switzerland, too, the conclusion has been reached that the change to the BA/MA has primarily served the purpose of expanding the bureaucratic apparatus but damaging the quality of education. On top of this, economists have been able to prove that the transformation of the higher education system has swallowed up funds that should have been invested in making education more egalitarian. If the Bologna Declaration is to be implemented in the national context without having a negative effect on educational equality, then the process will need to be prolonged, coordinated and democratic.

'BOLOGNA' IN THE CONTEXT OF TRANSFORMED STATEHOOD

On the one hand, the introduction of the BA/MA system in the German-language space corresponds to the interests of national governments who can make cuts in the education system and in teaching staff while appealing to the European-led reform process. The introduction of tuition fees is also often legitimised through precisely the same appeal to the Bologna Reforms: an example of the political instrumentalisation of the process. On the whole, however, the implementation of the Bologna declaration and the boundless bureaucratisation that goes with it has demonstrated retrogressive traits.

On the other hand, this new form of 'governance' illustrates the way in which national governments are being confronted with a new form of statehood, where supra-state actors exercise an increasing influence over national legislation. This is by no means restricted only to education policy as the anti-globalisation movement has made clear. What enables these supra-state specifications to be implemented is above all a highly abstract discourse appealing to the regulatory power of the free market and to the need for competitiveness, efficiency and optimisation – in other words to neoliberal ideologies. The goals of the Bologna Process are therefore also to be placed in the context of the post-national politics of the European Union, and indicate a whole new dynamic of inclusion and exclusion that does not only exist in higher education. The background to this turn is the assumption that learning processes play a dominant role in creating differentiated markets in global competition. The knowledge to be produced in the restructured universities is based on the assumption that knowledge can be accelerated and optimised, that access to it can be controlled via patenting and monetisation and also that knowledge can only be coupled to concrete uses, for example the economic success of companies.[10] The production and distribution of knowledge is to be re-ordered according to the principles of salesmanship.

At the same time, the paradoxes between supra-state and national agendas have opened up a new process of negotiation that recognises the discrepancies between programme, discourse, interpretation and praxis on the European and national levels. This process has enabled a broad critique of the creeping economisation and de-democratisation in the German-language space and given rise to a transnational protest movement.

BROADENING PERSPECTIVES: A CRITIQUE OF THE MIGRATION REGIME

The critique of the university reforms and the discussion about the mobility of the privileged in the economy of knowledge must nevertheless broaden its perspectives to include both the European border and migration regime and the post-colonial critique of Eurocentrism in the content of knowledge and the methods with which it is produced. While younger generations of academics are increasingly recruited from emerging nations because of the relaxation of the restrictive immigration laws of the European nation-states and via new forms of 'education marketing', the access of non EU-countries to Europe is becoming increasingly difficult. For example, the German immigration law of 2005 anticipates a hierarchy between 'qualified' and 'non-qualified', while the UNESCO Global Education Digest from 2006 shows that, on an international scale, it is increasingly the case that only those considered to be 'highly qualified' are issued with a residence permit. According to the latest statistics, the emigration of highly educated, scientific and technical university staff to countries supposedly better equipped for education and research has also begun to be an issue for countries in northern Europe.[11] Most affected, however, are countries whose education system is still marked and disadvantaged by the history of European colonialism. The countries who profit from the so-called 'brain drain', meanwhile, are above all the English speaking nations: the USA, Canada, Australia and England.

At the time of writing, universities throughout Europe and the US are being occupied. In Austria, the protests that started at the Academy of Fine Arts in Vienna have spread throughout the country and students and teachers are expressing their solidarity with the international strikes in higher education. Among the issues being criticised by the protest movement are restrictions on access, the under-funding of universities, the demotion of university education to mere schooling and the introduction of tuition fees. Also among the protesters' concerns are the post-Bologna European university reforms and the way they have been propagated and implemented at the national level over the last decade. The protests have highlighted the contradictions between the national and the supranational goals of the university reforms. These struggles have to be taken on in the context of the EU's isolationist politics and need to become truly transnational.

NOTES

1. These reflections are a result of the project <reformpause> presented at the Kunstraum University of Lüneburg, Germany, 2006. The project <reformpause> was generated by myself (Marion von Osten) in collaboration with the cultural studies student group including Christiane Autsch, Kristina Geertz, Ludmila Gerasimov, Julia Hammer, Rahel-Katharina Hermann, Katharina Looks, Jenny Nachtigall, Maria Petersen, Kathrin Roes, Stephanie Schneider, Frauke Schnoor, Stephanie Seidel, Valentina Seidel, Nike Thurn and Anna Till.

2. Ivan Illich, 'Commencement at the University of Puerto Rico', *New York Review of Books*, 13 (6), 9 October 1969.

3. Ivan Illich, *Celebration of Awareness: A Call for Institutional Revolution* (Garden City, NY: Doubleday, 1970), p. 121.

4. Georg Picht, *Die deutsche Bildungskatastrophe*, Olten and Freiburg, 1964.

5. Abitur is a designation used in Germany and Finland for final exams that young adults take at the end of their secondary education, usually after 12 or 13 years of schooling.

6. See André Gorz (ed.), *Schule und Fabrik* (Internationale Marxistische Diskussion 30) (Berlin: Merve, 1972).

7. See Paola Melchiori, *Free University of Women. Reflections on the Conditions for a Feminist Politics of Knowledge* (Bingley: Emerald Group, 2006), pp. 125–44.

8. Prager Kommuniqué, 'Auf dem Wege zum europäischen Hochschulraum', 19 May 2001. Available at: http://www.bmbf. de/pub/prager_kommunique.pdf [accessed 22 January 2011].

9. See BMWF, *Bericht über den Stand der Umsetzung der Bologna Ziele in Österreich* 2009, p. 19. Available at: http://bmwf.gv.at/ uploads/tx_contentbox/bologna-bericht_2009.pdf [accessed 22 January 2011].

10. See Yann Moulier-Boutang, 'Neue Grenzziehungen in der politischen Ökonomie', in Marion von Osten (ed), *Norm der Abweichung* (Zürich/Wien/New York: Voldemeer/Springer, 2003).

11. UNESCO, *Global Education Digest 2006. Comparing Education Statistics Across the World* (Montreal: UNESCO Institute for Statistics, 2006).

16

International Students and the Globalization of Higher Education

Kirsten Forkert

International students in the UK play a contradictory, and increasingly controversial, role within both the marketisation of education and the control of borders. They function as 'cash cows' (as they have paid significantly higher fees than European students), 'guinea pigs' for various market research and auditing tools and, more recently, as 'scapegoats' (as in the current moral panic surrounding 'bogus students' and 'terror suspects'). Crucially, they are *not seen as learners*. Their situation thus raises many questions about the fate and nature of the higher education (HE) sector in the UK, as well as other issues around civil liberties and freedom of movement. This chapter focuses in particular on how discourses and policies that position international students as *commodities* contribute to making their rights and civil liberties more contingent – and how this then makes them vulnerable to the negative effects of policy reforms designed to prove that the government is being 'tough on immigration'. It ends by calling for greater analysis of the connections between neoliberalism and xenophobia and for solidarity between campaigns against cuts and immigration controls.

INTERNATIONAL STUDENTS AS CASH COWS: 'THE SONS AND DAUGHTERS OF SHEIKS'?

One of the ways in which international students are framed by media and policy discourses is as 'cash cows', who are accepted to UK universities because they pay significantly higher fees than European students.[1] Non-EU students now make up more than 10 per cent of the entire student population and their fees provide 9 per cent of the total revenue of higher education. Income to universities from international students has already risen from £455 million in 1995 to £2.2 billion in 2009[2] and yet, as a result of the financial uncertainty caused by the cuts (even with increased home fees), many institutions are hoping to raise still further the quota of international students. This will, of course, not be a straightforward process as the government simultaneously intends to restrict the number of students allowed in the country as part of its plans to cap immigration.[3]

The academic work of international students, however, is often seen to be of substandard quality and they are held to be at least partly responsible for the 'dumbing down' of education precisely because of the perception that they are accepted to British universities for purely economic, rather than academic, reasons. The 'cash cow' stereotype is also connected to the characterisation of international students as spoiled rich kids (which pre-dates the charging of higher fees, and which may have served as justification for their introduction).

Higher fees for international students were actually introduced in the 1980s, provoking widespread student protest. In an article in the *Guardian* on tuition fees, Jonathan Wolff mentions an interview with pre-Thatcher Labour cabinet member Andrew Lever about the decision. Lever argued that that the UK government should not subsidise the 'sons and daughters of sheiks', claiming that the 'cost of studying in the UK ... was already beyond the purse of all but the most privileged' and so international students would not be deterred by higher fees.[4] Lever's comment reflects both the perception of international students as wealthy and also an underlying belief that the British government should not 'subsidise foreigners'. Both these views continue to be prevalent within media and policy networks, and they are central to current and recent immigration reforms.

Following the increase in fees for international students, in 1999 the then Labour government launched the Prime Minister's Initiative (PMI), as part of a five-year strategy to increase the number of international students in the UK, effectively paving the way for the marketisation of international education. According to Beatrice Merrick, director of services and research for the UK Council for International Student Affairs (UKCISA), one of the organisations charged with implementing the initiative:

> The launch of the Prime Minister's Initiative for International Education in 1999 marked something of a watershed in UK international educational policy. For the first time, there was recognition at the highest political level of the importance of *the international higher education industry* to the UK. Competitor countries around the world looked on with interest and used the PMI as a lever to persuade their own governments of the need to develop international educational strategies – and to provide (or increase) budgets to go with them.[5]

The goal of the PMI was to develop overseas markets and revenue streams for British colleges and universities whose traditional sources of funding (state support) were and are being systematically undone. It marked a shift from a model of HE as a national public good to a global commodity, subject to the pressures of international competition (an international public good was inconceivable within this context). Underlying this policy shift was a belief on the part of the Department for Business, Innovation and Skills (BIS) that universities as institutions must do more to contribute to an economic agenda. In this context international students constitute a 'solution' for governments who want a 'world class' HE system without sufficient levels of public investment. This situation positions international students as economic resources and indexes of global competitiveness; their value to British society is defined almost exclusively in economic terms.

INTERNATIONAL STUDENTS AS GUINEA PIGS

This framing of international students as economic resources rather than learners also coincides with the increasing prevalence of auditing systems within education, as well as the role of private contractors in administering these systems. Market research tools are used to measure and monitor the experience of international students, defined narrowly in 'customer satisfaction' terms. One of these tools is the International Student Barometer (ISB), developed by the Graduate Insight Group, or i-graduate, a London-based multinational company with offices in the UK, the USA, Australia and Amsterdam. It bills the International Student Barometer, currently in use in 190 countries, as 'the largest annual study of international student experience in the world'.[6] Offering a cash prize of up to £1,000, the survey invites international students to report on their perceptions and expectations of their study. The data can be used to assess the educational provider's national and global competitiveness.

What is more insidious, however, is the ISB's role as a mechanism of performance evaluation. Client testimonials on the i-graduate website reveal that the survey results are used to provide 'positive reinforcement' for staff 'when they are doing well' but also to identify 'major gaps in their understanding of internationalisation' and to provide 'a barometer of how they should plan their curriculum to suit a global perspective'.[7] In this way, the ISB can be used by HE management to predict and control the behaviour of both international students and staff, contributing to the (further) manipulation and exploitation of international students, and to the loss of autonomy for academic staff. After the success of the ISB, i-graduate then decided to introduce, and market the Student Barometer for European students. Does this reflect a situation where international students pilot market research tools which are then adopted in HE on a wider scale?

INTERNATIONAL STUDENTS AS SCAPEGOATS: 'BOGUS STUDENTS' AND 'TERROR SUSPECTS'

More recently, stories about 'bogus students' who are in the country not to study but to work have become common within media and pressure group discourses.[8] The media hysteria around Umar Farouk Abdulmutallab, the 'Detroit bomber', raised the spectre of the international student as 'terror suspect' who is 'radicalised' through Islamic student societies and/or uses study as a cover for terrorist activity.[9] These perceptions frame the presence and activities of international students as essentially fraudulent and potentially dangerous. For example, part-time employment (to which students are legally entitled, paying income tax and National Insurance contributions on their earnings) becomes seen as illegitimate and even immoral, as 'stealing jobs' from unemployed British youth. Because international students are also assumed to be spoiled rich kids, the idea that they might need to work in order to pay high tuition fees is never considered. The term 'overstaying' (which technically means being in the country without a valid visa), has been also applied to students who legitimately remain in the country for work or marriage purposes.[10] Compounded by the lack of international student representation in the media, this situation then makes it very easy for governments to play to populist politics by restricting the rights, entitlements and civil liberties of international students with little public opposition. This has resulted in a raft of policy measures to monitor and control international students' activities.

One of these policies, the Points Based System of Immigration (PBSI), was introduced in March 2009. Tier 4 of PBSI that deals specifically with student visas requires universities to be licensed by the Home Office in order to sponsor international students to study in the UK. They are also required to monitor and report[11] on their students' activities. Universities are awarded differential status based on their track record and compliance with UKBA regulations. 'Highly trusted sponsors' (HTS) are those 'who have the highest levels of compliance with their sponsor obligations, and whose students are showing the greatest compliance with the terms of their visa or permission to stay'.[12]

Under the new proposals international students are to be part of the planned immigration cap, and are to be subject to differential financial requirements depending on whether their country of origin is classified as 'high risk' or 'low risk', a move which led even the UKBA to admit that such an approach 'is likely to require an exemption from the Race Relations Act'.[13]

Discussing the proposed restrictions in detail is outside the scope of this chapter, but they also include limiting students' access to pre-sessional courses (such as language courses), raising the language requirements, making it more difficult for students to stay after their studies (through the scrapping of the Post-Study Work scheme), and limiting both their ability to work and bring dependents.[14] These shifts in immigration policy mark the entry of discourses and agendas of security and border control (the mandate of the Home Office) into higher education. Underlying these shifts is a belief on the part of the Home Office that universities must do more to contribute to a security agenda, and that international students constitute a 'problem' in so far as they (as a social/political category) travel to the UK with the primary intention of 'abusing the system'.

If international students are positioned as a problem in certain respects, in other ways they ironically also constitute a 'solution' for neoliberal governments in detracting from cuts to public services and rationalising the imposition of further systems of control on previously public institutions. International students are depicted as exploiting the UK's generosity and hospitality, rather than being exploited by the burden of very high tuition fees or visa application fees which, at the time of writing, are £357 for an application by post and £650 in person. Whereas historically, immigrants were exploited for their labour, international students are now primarily exploited for their investment. At the same time as these developments, state-funded scholarship schemes for international students have been terminated, including the Overseas Student Research Award (ORSAS) a long-running initiative set up by the Secretary of State for Education and Science. We can see the withdrawal of these scholarships as symptomatic of a discourse that positions students less as learners and increasingly as frauds and security threats, making public investment in these schemes controversial. Importantly, however, these shifts have not gone unopposed. Campaigns such as Students Not Suspects, comprised of a coalition of staff, students, and civil liberties campaigners working together to draw attention to the impact of PBIS, have been active since 2009 and have organised a series of public events to draw attention to the issues.[15]

CONNECTIONS BETWEEN NEOLIBERALISM AND XENOPHOBIA

It is important to consider the links between marketising and securitising discourses, and the role of international students within both. Why, for example, is it not so great a leap from thinking of international students as cash cows to thinking of them as security threats? If universities in the UK are structurally dependent on the high fees paid by international students, and their compliance with immigration regimes, then surely what needs to be questioned is this structural dependence. We also need to examine neoliberalism and xenophobia as ideologies that frame education and mobility as individual privileges (for those who meet criteria based on high income and market-determined skills), not as universal rights based on the need to meaningfully participate in contemporary life.

Within the current climate of cuts, we also need to understand these immigration reforms as making access to any publicly funded services increasingly contingent. Through these reforms, the neoliberal imperative to restrict access to public service dovetails with longer-standing forms of xenophobia, particularly the perception, mentioned at the beginning of this chapter, that foreigners are a drain on the system and so should not be subsidised. In the face of these pressures, linking campaigns against cuts and campaigns against immigration controls has become particularly urgent. Fundamental questions need to be asked about the necessity of both cuts to public services and also the immigration cap, and why alternatives are not being taken seriously.

The situation of international students also brings up certain unresolved contradictions around the perceived responsibilities of governments (as serving the citizens of their own nation only) within a global environment where people move for work or study reasons. Related to this, more work needs to be done to bring on board those individuals and groups who may implicitly support immigration controls as a means of slowing down or stopping the marketisation of HE. It is also important to publicly challenge discourses within the emerging anti-cuts movement that would appeal to narrow and nostalgic definitions of working-class identity which are seen to be against the interests of international students and to develop solidarities amongst international students, British students and staff. Finally, what are urgently needed are analyses with the imagination and audacity to re-frame teaching and learning as an international public good, one that is simultaneously cross-border and oriented not only towards professional success, but towards individual and collective transformation.

NOTES

1. Mike Reddin, 'International fees for undergraduate students 2009–2010', *Guardian*, 8 November 2009. Available at: http://www.guardian.co.uk/education/table/2009/oct/08/undergraduate-international-student-fees [accessed 24 January 2011].

2. Universities UK, *Higher education facts and figures*, summer 2010 (London: UUK, 2010), pp. 7, 15, 16.

3. UKBA, 'Government sets out proposals for major reform of the student visa system', press release, 7 December 20120. Available at: http://www.ukba.homeoffice.gov.uk/sitecontent/newsarticles/2010/dec/16student-visa-system [accessed 25 January 2011].

4. JonathanWolff, 'How did we get into this mess over fees?', *Guardian*, 1 September 2009.

5. Beatrice Merrick, 'Preparation for success: key themes in the prime minister's initiative on international education', paper presented at the 2007 ISANA International Conference, 'Student success in international education', 27–30 November, Adelaide, Australia. Available at: http://www.isana.org.au/files/isana07final00049.pdf [accessed October 1, 2010]. Emphasis added.

6. i-graduate testimonials. Available at: http://www.i-graduate.org/testimonials/ [accessed 29 September 2010].

7. Ibid.

8. MigrationWatch, *The Cost of Bogus Students*, 4 January 2011. Available at: http://www.migrationwatchuk.org/briefingPaper/document/216 [accessed 24 January 2011]; Richard Watson, 'UK Visa System Fraud Exposed', BBC *Newsnight*, 24 February 2010. Available at: http://news.bbc.co.uk/1/hi/programmes/newsnight/8528781.stm [accessed: 24 January 2011].

9. Gordon Rayner, 'Detroit bomber: British university "complicit" in radicalisation', *Daily Telegraph*, 30 December 2009.

10. Karen McVeigh, 'One in five overseas students remains in UK after five years, Home Office report shows', *Guardian*, 6 September 2010.

11. Although student attendance has been recorded for some time by university departments for pastoral reasons, as part of their duty of care as institutions, this information has not been required to be passed on to government agencies such as the UKBA.

12. Universities UK and the UK Council for International Student Affairs (UKCISA) both lobbied against the HTS scheme on the grounds that it conflated immigration compliance with academic excellence and had the potential to damage universities' international reputation. See John Morgan, 'UUK warns members off signing up to visa sponsor scheme', *Times Higher Education Supplement*, 29 April 2010.

13. Geoffrey Alderman, 'An immigration bar too far', *Times Higher Education Supplement*, 13 January 2011.

14. Ruth Grove-White, 'What's looming for international students? New government consultation outlines latest set of proposals, Migrants' Rights Network, 10 December 2010. Available at: http://www.migrantsrights.org.uk/blog/2010/12/whats-looming-international-students-new-government-consultation-outlines-latest-set-pr [accessed 31 January 2011].

15. See the Students Not Suspects website, available at: http://www.studentsnotsuspects.blogspot.com [accessed 25 January 2011].

Part VI

The Manifesto

DEMANDS ON GOVERNMENT

- Increase proportion of UK public expenditure devoted to higher education to at least the EU19 average of 1.1 per cent (up from 0.7 per cent) – a move that would bring in billions of pounds to the sector.
- Restoration of maintenance grants and abolition of fees to be paid for through an increase in corporation tax and an increase to the top level of personal income tax.
- Restoration of the block grant for all subjects.
- Scrapping of the Research Excellence Framework (REF) and its replacement with a way of monitoring research work based on respect for the ability of individuals and groups of researchers to define their own research aims and priorities.
- Scrapping of the National Student Survey and other forms of evaluation which perpetuate cultures of 'customer satisfaction' and quality control, and their replacement with forms of feedback that encourage meaningful reflection on teaching and learning.
- Scrapping of the Points Based System of Immigration as it affects the higher education sector and a halt to punitive measures affecting the free movement of international staff and students.
- Ending the requirement of international students to pay significantly higher tuition fees than European students and thus their role as 'cash cows'.

DEMANDS ON UNIVERSITIES

- Commitment by employers to nationally agreed terms and conditions for all staff and recognition of trade unions to negotiate these terms and conditions.
- Commitment by employers to address the gender pay gap with immediate effect.
- A commitment to staff/student ratios at the OECD average or better.

- Commitment by employers to move away from the use of hourly-paid contracts for teachers and to offer permanent contracts after two consecutive years of teaching.
- Salaries of senior staff and vice-chancellors to be fixed as part of a nationally agreed scale with an income differential, as suggested by Citizens UK, of no more than a multiple of ten.
- Universities to adopt mission statements, relevant to each institution, that recognise the obligation of institutions to foster independent and critical thought, to ensure access to the university for all social groups, and to seek the participation of the local community in the life of the university.
- Democratisation of governing bodies through the allocation of equal votes to staff and student representatives, community members, and employers' representatives.
- An end wherever possible to the outsourcing of university services including catering, cleaning, international student recruitment, and sickness absence reporting; where outsourcing does take place, a commitment only to consider companies who recognise trade unions and who pay a Living Wage.
- Commitment by employers to affordable, on-campus childcare provision.
- Extension of the remit of research ethics committees to consider, with teeth, the ethics of research for the arms trade, the military and the nuclear industry.
- Pledge by universities not to accept donations from individuals or regimes that refuse to sign a statement on academic freedom that guarantees the right of academics and researchers in the 'donor' countries to teach and research without fear of state intervention.

SIGNATORIES TO THE MANIFESTO

Nadje Al-Ali, SOAS, University of London
Etienne Balibar, Université de Paris-Nanterre

Ted Benton, University of Essex
Bruno Bosteels, Cornell University
Wendy Brown, University of California, Berkeley
Pat Caplan, Goldsmiths, University of London
Pat Carlen, Editor, *British Journal of Criminology*
John Clarke, Open University
John Corner, University of Leeds
James Curran, Goldsmiths, University of London
Mike Cushman, Secretary LSE UCU
Nick Davies, author
Jeremy Dear, President, National Union of Journalists
Peter Dews, University of Essex
European Group for the Study of Deviance and Social Control
Mark Fisher, Goldsmiths, University of London
Nancy Fraser, New School for Social Research, New York
Valerie Fraser, University of Essex
Jeremy Gilbert, University of East London
Paul Gilroy, London School of Economics
Dave Gordon, University of Bristol
Lawrence Grossberg, University of North Carolina
Sylvia Harvey, University of Leeds
Dick Hobbs, University of Essex
Fred Inglis, University of Sheffield
Ernesto Laclau, University of Essex
Neal Lawson, chair of Compass
Colin Leys, Queen's University, Canada
Michael Lowy, National Center for Scientific Research (CNRS), Paris
Knut Lundby, University of Oslo
Ben Manski, Democratizing Education Network, former co-chair US Green Party
Philip Marfleet, University of East London
Scott McCracken, Keele University
John McDonnell MP
Angela McRobbie, Goldsmiths, University of London
Sam Mejias, President, Institute of Education Students' Union
China Mieville, author
David Miller, University of Strathclyde

Toby Miller, University of California, Riverside
Chantal Mouffe, University of Westminster
Graham Murdock, Loughborough University
Karma Nabulsi, Oxford University
Chris Newfield, University of California, Santa Barbara
Cary Nelson, President, American Association of University
    Professors
Alex Peters-Day, General Secretary LSE Students Union
Michael Pickering, Loughborough University
John Pilger, writer and broadcaster
Ken Plummer, University of Essex
Malcolm Povey, University of Leeds
Nina Power, Roehampton University
Sean Rillo Raczka, Vice President, University of London Union
Hilary Rose, London School of Economics
Steven Rose, The Open University
Andrew Ross, New York University
David Rushton, Institute of Local Television and University of
    Strathclyde
Alfredo Saad Filho, SOAS, University of London
Richard Sennett, London School of Economics
Michael J. Shapiro, University of Hawaii and The European
    Graduate School
Bev Skeggs, Goldsmiths, University of London
Neil Smith, University of Aberdeen
Clare Solomon, President University of London Union 2010/11
Tiziana Terranova, Università degli Studi di Napoli L'Orientale
Paul Thompson, University of Essex
Steve Tombs, John Moores University
Wendy Wheeler, London Metropolitan University

And approximately 500 other academics and researchers

Notes on Contributors

Michael Bailey teaches sociology at Essex University. Publications include: *Narrating Media History* (2009), *Mediating Faiths: Religion and Socio-Cultural Change in the Twenty-First Century* (edited with Guy Redden, 2011), *Richard Hoggart: Culture and Critique* (edited with Mary Eagleton, 2011) and *Understanding Richard Hoggart: A Pedagogy of Hope* (with Ben Clarke and John Walton, 2011).

Nick Couldry is Professor of Media and Communications at Goldsmiths, University of London and director of the Centre for the Study of Global Media and Democracy. He is the author or editor of nine books including *The Place of Media Power: Pilgrims and Witnesses of the Media Age* (2000), *Inside Culture* (2000), *Media Rituals: A Critical Approach* (2003), and most recently, *Why Voice Matters: Culture and Politics After Neoliberalism* (2010).

Aeron Davis is a Reader in Political Communication at Goldsmiths, University of London. He is the author of three books and some 30 articles on a range of subjects, including political parties and government, business and finance, trade unions and interest groups, media and communication.

Neil Faulkner is an Honorary Research Fellow in the Department of Archaeology and Anthropology at the University of Bristol, a Fellow of the Society of Antiquaries, and the Co-director of the Great Arab Revolt Project and the Sedgeford Historical and Archaeological Research Project. He is a member of the Coalition of Resistance Steering Committee, a member of the Counterfire Editorial Board, and the author of *A Marxist History of the World*, which is being serialised on the Counterfire website.

Natalie Fenton is Professor of Communications in the Department of Media and Communications at Goldsmiths, University of London, co-director of the Goldsmiths Leverhulme Media Research Centre and editor or author of *New Media, Old News: Journalism and Democracy in the Digital Age* (2010), *Journalism and Democracy in the Digital Age* (2010) and *New Media and Radical Politics* (forthcoming).

Kirsten Forkert is a researcher and activist, currently completing a PhD at Goldsmiths, University of London.

Des Freedman is Reader in Communications and Cultural Studies at Goldsmiths, University of London. He is the author or editor of *The Politics of Media Policy*, *Television Policies of the Labour Party*, *War and the Media: Reporting Conflict 24/7* (with Daya Thussu), *Protecting the News: Civil Society and the Media* (with Tamara Witschge and Natalie Fenton). He is secretary of the Goldsmiths branch of the UCU.

Henry A. Giroux holds the Global TV Network Chair in English and Cultural Studies at McMaster University in Canada. His most recent books include: *The University in Chains: Confronting the Military–Industrial–Academic Complex* (2007), *Youth in a Suspect Society: Democracy or Disposability?* (2009), *Politics Beyond Hope* (2010), *Hearts of Darkness: Torturing Children in the War on Terror* (2010); *Zombie Politics and Culture in the Age of Casino Capitalism* (2011).

Feyzi Ismail is a PhD student at the School of Oriental and African Studies (SOAS). She was central to the SOAS occupation and appeared in the media defending the student protests. She is a regular contributor to Counterfire.org.

Jon Nixon is Honorary Professor of Educational Studies at the University of Sheffield, UK. He has previously held chairs at four UK universities. His recent and forthcoming publications include: *Towards the Virtuous University: the Moral Bases of Academic Professionalism* (2008), *Transforming Learning in Schools and Communities: the Remaking of Education for a Cosmopolitan Society* (edited with Bob Lingard and Stewart Ranson, 2008), *Higher Education and the Public Good: Imagining the University* (2011), *Interpretive Pedagogies for Higher Education: Arendt, Berger, Said, Nussbaum and their Legacies* (forthcoming), and (edited with Bob Adamson and Feng Su) *The Reorientation of Higher Education: Compliance and Defiance* (forthcoming). He is currently engaged in a study of *Hannah Arendt and Radical Friendship*.

Marion von Osten is a founding member of Labor k3000, kpD (kleines post-fordistisches Drama), and the Centre for Post-Colonial Knowledge and Culture, Berlin. Her main research interests concern the working conditions of cultural production in post-colonial societies, technologies of the self, and the governance of mobility.

John Rees is the writer and presenter of the political history series *Timeline* and an editorial board member of the online magazine *Counterfire*. Previous books include *The Algebra of Revolution* and *Imperialism and Resistance*. He was a co-founder of both the Stop the War Coalition and the Coalition of Resistance.

Nick Stevenson is a Reader in Cultural Sociology, University of Nottingham. His most recent books include *Education and Cultural Citizenship* (2011), *David Bowie* (2006), *Cultural Citizenship* (2003), *Culture and Citizenship* (2002), *Understanding the Media* (2001) and *Making Sense of Men's Lifestyle Magazines* (2001). He is currently working on a book called *Freedom* for publication by Routledge in 2012.

Alberto Toscano teaches in the Department of Sociology at Goldsmiths, University of London and is the author of *'Fanaticism': A Brief History of the Concept* (2010). He is also on the editorial board of the journal *Historical Materialism*.

John K. Walton is an IKERBASQUE Research Professor in the Department of Contemporary History, University of the Basque Country, Spain. He is a historian of tourism, regional identities, sport and the Co-operative movement, and edits the *Journal of Tourism History*. His most recent book (with Keith Hanley) is *Constructing Cultural Tourism: John Ruskin and the Tourist Gaze* (2010).

Index

Compiled by Sue Carlton